DISCOVERING THE PAST

DISCOVERING

MEDIEVAL REALMS

Colin Shephard
Alan Large

JOHN MURRAY

Acknowledgements

Illustrations by David Anstey; Peter Bull Art Studio; Art Construction; John Lupton/Linden Artists; Chris Rothero/Linden Artists.

Further illustrations reproduced by kind permission of: **p.23** Wharram Research Project; **p.83** from *A New Scottish History* by Melvin, Gould and Thompson, John Murray.

Photographs reproduced by kind permission of:
cover: British Library, London. **p.1** British Library; **p.2** *top left* The Pierpont Morgan Library, New York M763 f.19v; *top right* The Hulton Deutsch Collection; *bottom left* Bodleian Library, Oxford, Ms. Rawl. D.410 f.1r; *centre and bottom right* British Library; **p.3** *top left* The Hulton Deutsch Collection; *top right* British Library; *bottom left* Michael Holford; *centre right* The Master and Fellows of Trinity College, Cambridge; *bottom right* Bodleian Library, Oxford, Ms. Bodl. 264 f. 121v; **p.4** L. and R. Adkins; **pp.6–15** *all* Michael Holford; **p.17** Dean and Chapter of Durham Cathedral; **p.20** *top* Cambridge University Collection: Crown Copyright 1991 MoD reproduced with the permission of the Controller of HMSO; *bottom* Michael Holford; **p.21** *top left* English Heritage; *top right* Walter Rawlings/Robert Harding Picture Library; **p.22** Cambridge University Collection: copyright reserved; **p.23** Peter Dunn/English Heritage; **p.24** British Library; **p.25** *top right* Bodleian Library, Oxford, Ms. Bodl. 763 f.80r; *bottom right* British Library; **p.26** *top* The Hulton Deutsch Collection; *bottom* AA Picture Library; **p.27** *both* British Library; **p.29** *all* British Library; **p.31** *top, bottom centre, bottom left and right* British Library; *top centre* The Bridgeman Art Library; **p.33** *all* British Library; **p.36** Peter Dunn/English Heritage; **p.37** Bodleian Library, Oxford, Ms. University College 165 p.8; **p.38** British Library; **p.39** *both* British Library; **p.43** *top* Scala; *bottom* British Library; **p.44** British Library; **p.45** *top* Michael Holford; *bottom* The Bridgeman Art Library; **p.46** Peter Bartlett/Ludlow Museum, Shropshire Museum Service; **p.47** AA Picture Library; **p.48** Ronald Sheridan/Ancient Art and Architecture Collection; **p.49** *top* Bibliothèque Arsenal, Paris/Photographie Bulloz; *bottom* British Library; **p.50** Michael Holford; **p.55** British Library; **p.56** Mary Evans Picture Library; **p.57** Public Record Office; **p.58** *top* British Library; *bottom* The Bridgeman Art Library; **p.60** Ronald Sheridan/Ancient Art and Architecture Collection; **p.61** Masters of the Bench of the Inner Temple/E.T. Archive; **pp.62–63** Scala; **pp.66–67** The President and Fellows of Corpus Christi College, Oxford/The Bodleian Library, Oxford, Ms. C.C.C. 157 pp.382–3; **pp.68–73** *all* British Library; **p.74** The Bridgeman Art Library; **p.76** *top* British Library; *centre* Windsor Castle, Royal Library, ©1991 H.M. the Queen; *bottom* House of Commons Public Information Office; **pp.79–80** *both* British Library; **p.83** The Master and Fellows of Corpus Christi College, Cambridge; **p.84** Windsor Castle, Royal Library, ©1991 H.M. the Queen; **p.85** Robert Harding Picture Library; **p.87** *top and bottom left* Michael Holford; *bottom right* Michael Jenner.

© Colin Shephard, Alan Large, 1993

First published 1991 as part of *Contrasts and Connections* by John Murray (Publishers) Ltd
50 Albemarle Street, London W1X 4BD

This edition first published 1993
Reprinted 1995, 1996, 1997, 1998, 1999, 2000

Typeset by Wearset, Boldon, Tyne & Wear
Printed in Hong Kong by Sheck Wah Tong Printing Press Ltd

A CIP catalogue record for this book is available from the British Library
Pupils' Book ISBN 0–7195–5177–3
Teacher's Evaluation Pack (pupils' book with 48pp teachers' notes) ISBN 0–7195–5178–1

THE SCHOOLS HISTORY PROJECT

This project was set up by the Schools Council in 1972. Its main aim was to suggest suitable objectives for History teachers, and to promote the use of appropriate materials and teaching methods for their realisation. This involved a reconsideration of the nature of History and its relevance in secondary schools, the design of a syllabus framework which shows the uses of History in the education of adolescents, and the setting up of appropriate examinations.

Since 1978 the project has been based at Trinity and All Saints' College, Leeds, where it is one of three curriculum development projects run and supported by the Centre for History Education. The project is now self funding and with the advent of the National Curriculum it has expanded its publications to provide courses throughout the Key Stages for pupils aged 5–16. The project provides INSET for all aspects of National Curriculum History.

Contents

N.B. Words in SMALL CAPITALS are defined in the glossary on page 92.

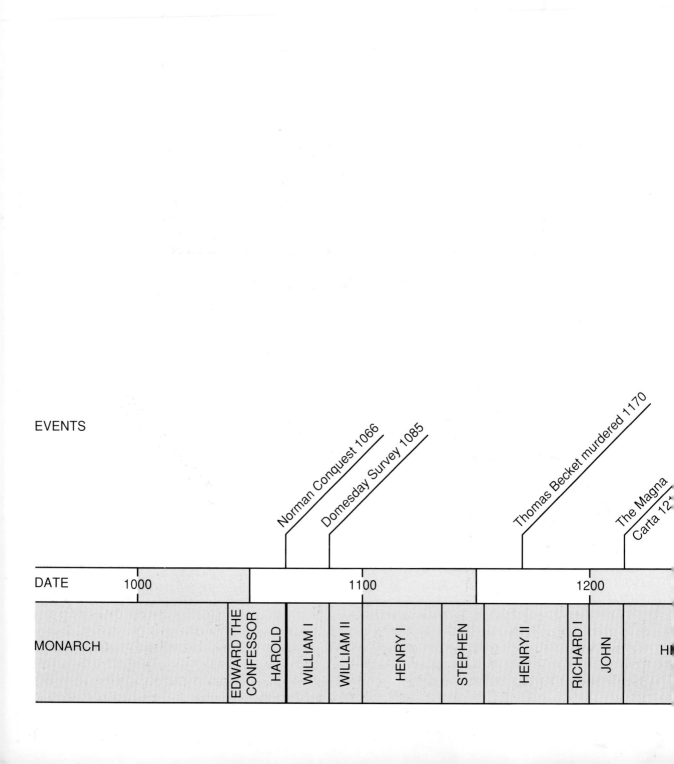

EVENTS

Norman Conquest 1066

Domesday Survey 1085

Thomas Becket murdered 1170

The Magna Carta 12·

DATE   1000   1100   1200

MONARCH   EDWARD THE CONFESSOR | HAROLD | WILLIAM I | WILLIAM II | HENRY I | STEPHEN | HENRY II | RICHARD I | JOHN | H

MEDIEVAL REALMS

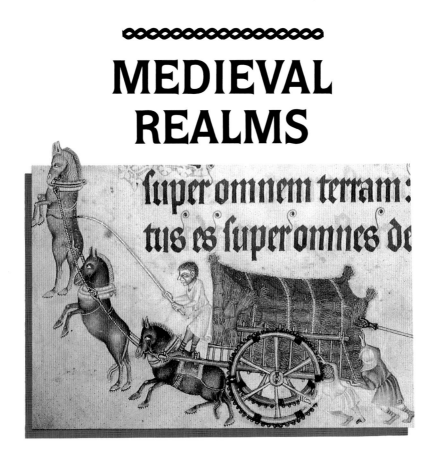

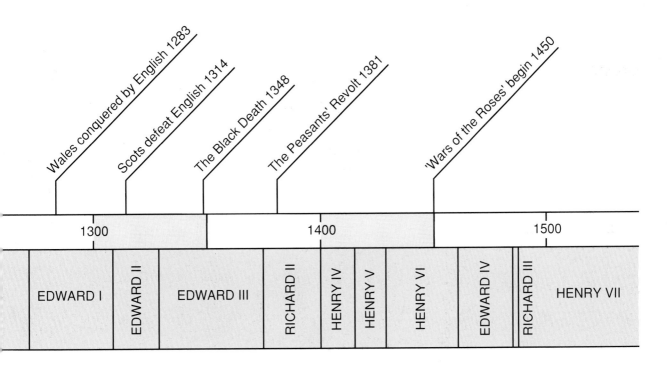

Wales conquered by English 1283

Scots defeat English 1314

The Black Death 1348

The Peasants' Revolt 1381

'Wars of the Roses' begin 1450

1300			1400					1500	
EDWARD I	EDWARD II	EDWARD III	RICHARD II	HENRY IV	HENRY V	HENRY VI	EDWARD IV	RICHARD III	HENRY VII

What were the Middle Ages like?

SOURCE 1 From a recent book about the Middle Ages

"*The medieval period began in 1066 when William of Normandy invaded England and defeated the English army at the Battle of Hastings. It continued full of battles and corpses until another battle in 1485 brought this violent period to a close.*"

LOOK at these two collections of sources. All the paintings come from the Middle Ages, and the photograph is of a church which was built during the Middle Ages. However, the two collections give very different impressions of what the Middle Ages were like.

After you have finished this unit on Medieval Realms, you will be able to make up your own mind about what the Middle Ages were like.

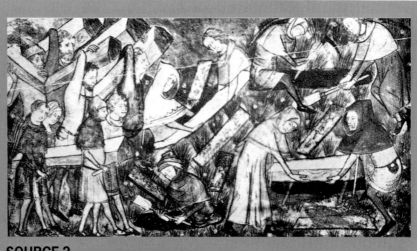

COLLECTION A

SOURCE 2

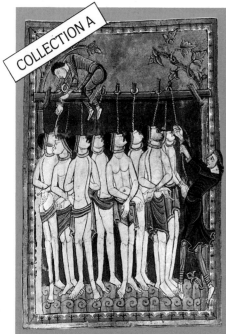

SOURCE 1

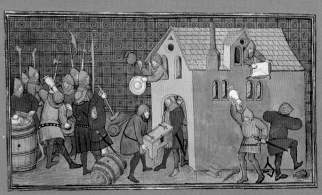

SOURCE 3

SOURCE 4

SOURCE 5

SOURCE 6

SOURCE 7

SOURCE 8

SOURCE 9

SOURCE 10

1. Explain what is happening in each of the sources in Collection A.
2. Use the sources in Collection A to write a description of what the Middle Ages were like.
   You could use some of these words in your description:

   peaceful   clever   dangerous
   cruel   violent   hardworking.
3. Explain what is happening in each of the sources in Collection B.

4. Use the sources in Collection B to write a description of what the Middle Ages were like. You could use some of the words in the list on the left in your description.
5. Historians disagree about what the Middle Ages were like. How do the two collections of sources help to explain why historians have different views of the Middle Ages?

England in the 1060s

ENGLAND in the 1060s was a very different place from England today. There were probably about $1\frac{1}{2}$ million people living in England, compared with 47 million today. Much of the southern half of the country was still covered by forest. Here and there were small villages where the forest had been cleared and the land was farmed. The northern and western parts of the country were even more thinly populated (see Source 1).

Nearly everyone worked on the land. There were few towns – probably only about twenty with a population of more than 1000. The largest of these towns are marked on Source 1.

England was governed by King Edward the Confessor, but he had trouble in keeping the country under control. Source 2 shows that England was divided into a number of earldoms, each ruled over by a powerful leader called an earl. These earls were meant to be loyal to the King, but sometimes they rebelled against him.

England was not a well defended country. There were hardly any castles, and most towns or villages were simply protected by earth embankments, like the ones shown in Source 3.

SOURCE 3 The remains of the earth embankments surrounding Wareham in Dorset

On the edge of Europe

England's connections with Scandinavia were much closer than with the rest of Europe. Earlier in the century, England had been part of the great VIKING EMPIRE of King Cnut of Denmark and Norway (see Source 4).

SOURCE 1 England's population in the 1060s. The largest towns are also shown

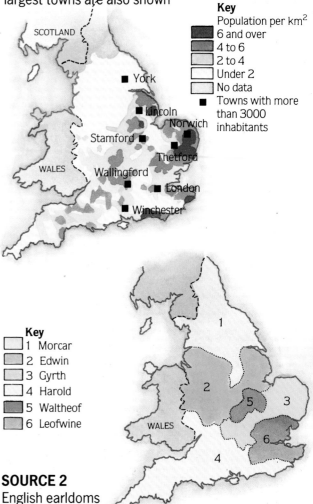

Key
Population per km^2
- 6 and over
- 4 to 6
- 2 to 4
- Under 2
- No data
- ■ Towns with more than 3000 inhabitants

Key
- 1 Morcar
- 2 Edwin
- 3 Gyrth
- 4 Harold
- 5 Waltheof
- 6 Leofwine

SOURCE 2
English earldoms

However, two developments were going to bring about much more contact between England and mainland Europe.

Across the English Channel, Normandy was a growing power. William, Duke of Normandy, had recently defeated some of the neighbouring countries. The Normans were even trying to conquer the island of Sicily. William also had ambitions to become King of England: if this happened England's connections with the rest of Europe would become much stronger.

England had one important thing in common with the rest of Europe. It was a Christian country and belonged to the Roman Catholic Church. The head of the Church was the Pope in Rome. He was in charge of all the BISHOPS and PRIESTS in England and the rest of the Christian countries of Europe – together known as Christendom.

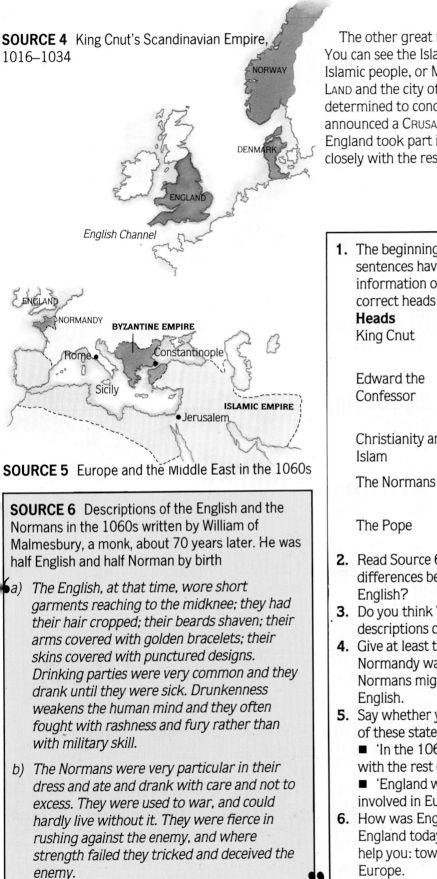

SOURCE 4 King Cnut's Scandinavian Empire, 1016–1034

English Channel

SOURCE 5 Europe and the Middle East in the 1060s

The other great religion at this time was ISLAM. You can see the Islamic Empire in Source 5. The Islamic people, or Muslims, had control of the HOLY LAND and the city of Jerusalem. The Pope was determined to conquer the Holy Land. In 1095 he announced a CRUSADE against the Muslims. If England took part it would mean co-operating closely with the rest of Europe.

1. The beginnings and endings of the following sentences have been mixed up. Using the information on these two pages, match the correct heads and tails.

Heads	Tails
King Cnut	were the two great religions of the time.
Edward the Confessor	wanted the European rulers to go on a Crusade to conquer the Holy Land.
Christianity and Islam	ruled over a great Scandinavian Empire.
The Normans	ruled over England in the 1060s.
The Pope	hoped to conquer England and Sicily.

2. Read Source 6 carefully. What were the differences between the Normans and the English?
3. Do you think William of Malmesbury's descriptions can be trusted?
4. Give at least three reasons why, if William of Normandy wanted to invade England, the Normans might find it easy to defeat the English.
5. Say whether you agree or disagree with each of these statements, and explain why:
   ▪ 'In the 1060s England had little contact with the rest of Europe.'
   ▪ 'England was likely to become more involved in Europe in the future.'
6. How was England in the 1060s different from England today? The following headings will help you: towns, religion, trade, contact with Europe.

SOURCE 6 Descriptions of the English and the Normans in the 1060s written by William of Malmesbury, a monk, about 70 years later. He was half English and half Norman by birth

a) *The English, at that time, wore short garments reaching to the midknee; they had their hair cropped; their beards shaven; their arms covered with golden bracelets; their skins covered with punctured designs. Drinking parties were very common and they drank until they were sick. Drunkenness weakens the human mind and they often fought with rashness and fury rather than with military skill.*

b) *The Normans were very particular in their dress and ate and drank with care and not to excess. They were used to war, and could hardly live without it. They were fierce in rushing against the enemy, and where strength failed they tricked and deceived the enemy.*

From across the water

THE month is September, the year 1066. It is early in the morning, about six o'clock. A boy and a girl sit near the ruins of the old Roman fort at Pevensey on the south coast of England. For a few moments they have escaped their daily chores.

After milking the family cow and eating a breakfast of warm milk and hard black bread, they have crept away to their favourite place on the cliffs to watch the dawn over the sea. It is getting lighter now and from their position on the cliffs they have a good view of the beach and the sea. The strong wind coming off the sea makes them shiver.

They are just about to leave when the girl notices some unfamiliar smudges on the horizon. What can they be? As the light grows stronger the smudges become clearer. They are ships, hundreds of them, and the wind is speeding them towards the beach.

Without knowing it, the boy and girl are seeing the beginning of one of the most important events in English history – the Norman Invasion.

SOURCE 1 This picture comes from the Bayeux Tapestry. The Normans had it embroidered in Kent in the 1070s to tell the story of their invasion of England

SOURCE 3 From the Bayeux Tapestry

SOURCE 4 From the Bayeux Tapestry

Captions

The Norman fleet approaches the coast of England

The Norman army lands

The Normans round up sheep and cows

The Normans prepare a feast

RVN: PRANDIVM: ET HIC EPIS
                 POTV: BE

NTVR: HIC:EST:VVAD AR D:

SOURCE 2   From the Bayeux Tapestry

IT   AD PEVENE   SÆ:-

1. Match the captions to the pictures in Sources 1–4.
2. List the pictures in the correct order.
3. Look carefully at Source 1.
   a) Describe how the two cooks (A) are cooking the meat.
   b) Why do you think the baker (B) is using a large pair of tongs?
   c) Can you see where the food is being taken indoors?
   d) Why is the table (C) made of shields?
   e) Why do you think this man (D) is blowing a horn?
4. Imagine you are the girl or boy watching the invasion from the old Roman fort. Describe the landing of the Norman army and what happens after they have landed. Try to include as much detail as you can find in Sources 1–4 about their ships, their clothing, their weapons and tools, and what they are doing.

IBVS:- ET HIC:MILITES: FESTINA   VERY ANT:HESTINGA: VT CIBVM. RAPERENT

Why was 1066 a year of crisis?

In 1066 England was invaded twice, there were two bloody battles for the English throne, and England had three different kings! Why was 1066 such a year of crisis in England?

One reason was that on 5 January 1066 the King of England, Edward the Confessor, died without any children. There were three people claiming to be the next King of England.

Edward's death certainly sparked off the crisis of 1066, but in fact trouble had been brewing for a long time. Edward had done well to stay in control of England until 1066. To understand why 1066 turned into such a year of violence, we must look at what had been happening during the years before.

SOURCE 1 England (including Wessex), Norway, Denmark and Normandy

NORWAY

DENMARK

ENGLAND

Wessex

NORMANDY

The Earls of Wessex

Harold Godwineson belonged to the most powerful family in England. They already controlled Wessex, but had ambitions to rule England. In 1051, Harold and his father rebelled against Edward, but were defeated and driven from the country. Harold returned the next year and soon became the most powerful nobleman in England. He thought he had the best claim to the throne because he was Edward's brother-in-law. Harold was also the only Englishman claiming the throne.

SOURCE 2 Written in about 1120 by a monk who was trained in Normandy

"While the crowds watched King Edward's funeral, Harold had himself crowned King alone by Archbishop Stigund, without the common consent of the other bishops and nobles. When the English learned that Harold had taken the throne they were moved to anger; some of the most powerful were ready to resist him by force."

SOURCE 3 From a book in praise of the Godwine family, written in 1066 by a foreign monk

"Archbishop Stigund whispered in Harold's ear that the King was broken with age and knew not what he said.
Stretching forth his hand to Harold, Edward said, 'I commend all the kingdom to your protection.'"

England and Normandy

When King Cnut invaded England in 1016, Edward the Confessor, who was then a young boy, fled to Normandy for protection. He stayed there until 1042, when he became King of England. As King, he had to protect his throne from Viking attacks and from the powerful Earls of Wessex.

In 1051 Harold Godwineson of Wessex rebelled against Edward. Edward asked his cousin **William, Duke of Normandy**, for help. William

1. Why did Harold Godwineson think he should be King of England?
2. Do you think his claim was a good one?

VBI HAROLD:SACRAMENTVM:FECIT:
VVILLELMO DVCI: HIC

England and Norway

In the 860s VIKINGS from Norway had invaded England and had settled in the north. In 1016 the Viking King Cnut had become King of England, Denmark and Norway. England was ruled by Norwegian kings until 1042, when the English Edward the Confessor seized the throne. The Norwegians planned two invasions in the 1040s, but they never happened.

The King of Norway in 1066 was **Harald Hardraada**. Harald wanted to rebuild the great Viking Empire of King Cnut. He also felt that he had a right to be King of England (see Source 4). He made raids on the English coast, and he planned a full-scale invasion of England. There were many people from Viking families in the north of England who might help him.

1. Why did Harald Hardraada think he should be King of England?
2. Do you think his claim was a good one?

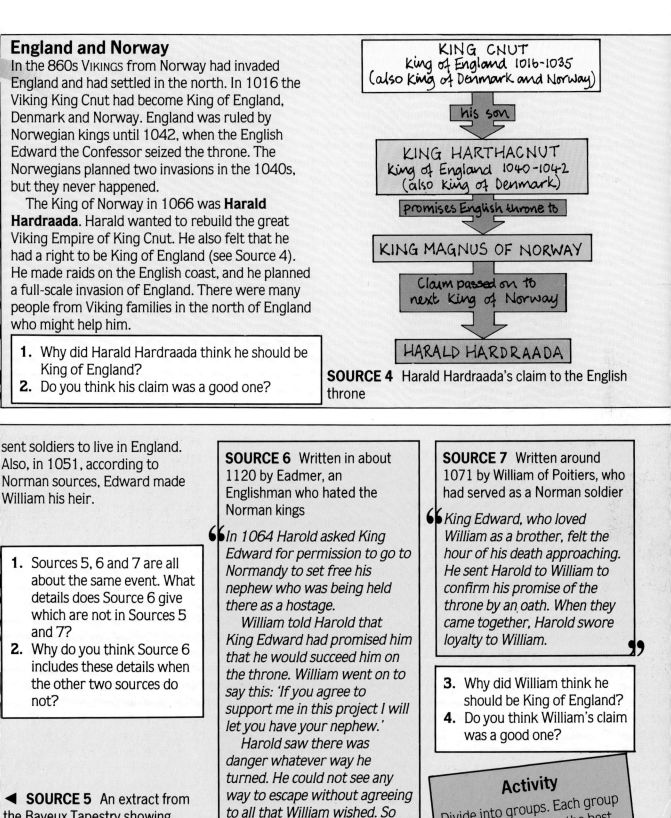

KING CNUT
King of England 1016–1035
(also King of Denmark and Norway)

his son

KING HARTHACNUT
King of England 1040–1042
(also King of Denmark)

promises English throne to

KING MAGNUS OF NORWAY

Claim passed on to next King of Norway

HARALD HARDRAADA

SOURCE 4 Harald Hardraada's claim to the English throne

---

sent soldiers to live in England. Also, in 1051, according to Norman sources, Edward made William his heir.

1. Sources 5, 6 and 7 are all about the same event. What details does Source 6 give which are not in Sources 5 and 7?
2. Why do you think Source 6 includes these details when the other two sources do not?

◄ **SOURCE 5** An extract from the Bayeux Tapestry showing Harold swearing his loyalty to William as the next King of England

SOURCE 6 Written in about 1120 by Eadmer, an Englishman who hated the Norman kings

❝In 1064 Harold asked King Edward for permission to go to Normandy to set free his nephew who was being held there as a hostage.

William told Harold that King Edward had promised him that he would succeed him on the throne. William went on to say this: 'If you agree to support me in this project I will let you have your nephew.'

Harold saw there was danger whatever way he turned. He could not see any way to escape without agreeing to all that William wished. So he agreed.❞

SOURCE 7 Written around 1071 by William of Poitiers, who had served as a Norman soldier

❝King Edward, who loved William as a brother, felt the hour of his death approaching. He sent Harold to William to confirm his promise of the throne by an oath. When they came together, Harold swore loyalty to William.❞

3. Why did William think he should be King of England?
4. Do you think William's claim was a good one?

Activity

Divide into groups. Each group must decide who has the best claim to the English throne. Prepare a wall display or poster to convince people that your candidate's claims are good ones.

Harold defends England

King Edward died on 5 January 1066. The next day, Harold Godwineson was crowned as king. But he must have known that he would have to fight both Harald Hardraada and William to stay king.

Throughout the summer of 1066 both William of Normandy and Harald Hardraada prepared their invasion fleets. Harold Godwineson prepared his defences and waited. William threatened the south coast, while Harald Hardraada threatened the north (see Source 8). Harold had to decide which coast to defend first.

The threat to the south coast

In January 1066 William started to build a fleet and gather his army together. By 12 August he was ready. He had 5000 foot-soldiers, and 2000 KNIGHTS on horseback. The most difficult part of the operation would be transporting these soldiers across the English Channel.

River Tyne

River Ouse

> Harold's brother Tosti lands with an invasion fleet of 60 ships May 1066.

SOURCE 8 Threats to Harold in 1066

SOURCE 9 Extracts from the Bayeux Tapestry showing William's preparations for the invasion

The wind was blowing in the wrong direction and so William waited. Harold Godwineson knew that William might invade at any moment.

William was not the only threat to the south coast. Tosti (Harold Godwineson's exiled brother) wanted revenge on Harold and had gathered together a fleet of 60 ships (see Source 10).

SOURCE 10 Written by Simeon of Durham a few years after the events it describes

> *Tosti landed at the Isle of Wight in May. After forcing the islanders to pay him money, he departed, and went along the south coast to the port of Sandwich, committing ravages. King Harold, who was then in London, ordered a large fleet and an army to be assembled. Tosti, being informed of this, withdrew.*
>
> *King Harold went to Sandwich and there waited for his fleet. When it had assembled, he went to the Isle of Wight, and as William was preparing to come with an army he kept watch the whole summer. But by 8 September provisions were growing scarce and Harold sent his navy and army home.*

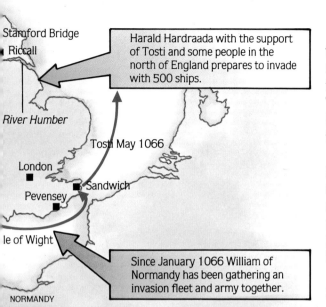

On the map:
Stamford Bridge
Riccall
Harald Hardraada with the support of Tosti and some people in the north of England prepares to invade with 500 ships.
River Humber
Tosti May 1066
London
Sandwich
Pevensey
Isle of Wight
NORMANDY
Since January 1066 William of Normandy has been gathering an invasion fleet and army together.

The threat to the north coast

Harald Hardraada had also been making preparations to invade. He had support from the people of the Orkneys, which belonged to him, and from Tosti and his fleet of ships, which had gone north. He also hoped for help from Malcolm, King of Scotland, and even from people in the north of England who were from VIKING families.

> **SOURCE 11** From an account by William of Malmesbury, written about 70 years after the events it describes
>
> In late May Tosti arrived on the Humber with a fleet of 60 ships, but was quickly driven away by Earl Edwin and Earl Morcar. He set sail for Scotland with only twelve ships. When he heard that Harald Hardraada was planning an attack on England with over 500 ships and 10,000 men, Tosti put himself under his command.

1. Put yourself in Harold Godwineson's position in the summer of 1066. You have news of William's invasion preparations, but you also know about Tosti and Harald Hardraada.
   - Do you guard the south coast?
   - Do you guard the north?
   - Do you split your forces and guard both?

   Explain carefully which course of action you would have taken. You must take into account who was the stronger, and who was likely to attack first.

On 18th September Harald Hardraada arrived at the mouth of the River Tyne with a powerful fleet of more than 500 ships. Earl Tosti joined him with his fleet. They sailed up the Ouse and landed at Riccall. The two brothers Earls Edwin and Morcar fought a battle with the Norwegians, but after a long fight the English fled. Many of them were killed.

Harold was now in a desperate position. After the long wait on the south coast he had just sent his soldiers and sailors home. He now had to gather his army together again, march hundreds of miles north, defeat the Norwegians and return south before the wind changed and allowed William to invade!

Source 12 tells us what then happened on 25 September.

> **SOURCE 12** From the Anglo-Saxon Chronicle, which was written by the English a long time after the events it describes. The writer was very much on Harold's side
>
> Then came our King Harold on the Norwegians unawares, and met them beyond York at Stamford with a great host of English folk; there was that day a very fierce battle fought on both sides. Harald Hardraada was killed, and Earl Tosti; the Norwegians that were left were put to flight, and the English fiercely struck them from behind, until some of them came to the ships. Some drowned, some were burnt, some died in various ways, so that there were few left. Only 24 ships returned to Norway.

This was a great victory for Harold against one of the greatest warriors of the time. But on the night of 27 September (two days later), the direction of the wind along the south coast changed and William's invasion fleet set sail. It landed at Pevensey, on the Sussex coast, early next morning.

Just think how Harold must have felt when he heard this news!

2. Harold had won a great victory in the north. Was his position now stronger or weaker than it was before Harald Hardraada's invasion?

11

Harold v. William: who will win?

LOOK at the timeline. It shows the events in the months and days leading up to the Battle of Hastings, and the different ways the two sides got ready for it.

As you study the timeline and all the sources on these two pages, remember that:

- William waited until the weather was suitable to cross the English Channel. He did not lose his patience and try to go too early.
- Harold had chosen to take the English throne and so was a target for both Harald Hardraada and William.
- Harold chose to guard the south coast and so had to dash up north quickly.
- Harold had to dash back from the north and attack William before he was really ready.

SOURCE 1 Written in about 1115 by Florence of Worcester, a monk

"Harold marched his army towards London by forced marches; and, although he knew that he had lost some of his best men in the recent battle, and that half of his troops were not yet assembled, he did not hesitate to meet the enemy.

William, Count of the Normans, had arrived with a countless host of horsemen, slingers, archers and foot-soldiers, and had brought with him also powerful help from all parts of France."

---

1. Looking at the timeline and all the sources on this page, which army do you think would be best prepared for the battle? Give reasons.

Movements in the months leading up to the battle

1066	Harold
May	Tosti attacks Isle of Wight. Harold guards south coast
July	
Aug 12	
Sept 8	Supplies for Harold's army and navy run out, and he sends them home
Sept 18	Harald Hardraada lands on Yorkshire coast with over 500 ships
Sept 20	Harald Hardraada defeats English earls at Fulford. Harold marching his army north
Sept 25	Harold defeats Harald Hardraada at Stamford Bridge
Sept 27	
Sept 28	
Sept 29	
Oct 2	Harold marches south (covering 50 miles a day), leaving many of his archers in the north
Oct 6	Harold reaches London and gathers together a new army, mainly foot-soldiers
Oct 11	Harold leaves London. Marches 58 miles towards Hastings
Oct 13	Harold arrives at Hastings during the night, with an army of 7000 exhausted men
Oct 14	THE BATTLE OF HASTINGS

William

- William continues to prepare his fleet: arms and people are gathered together

- Fleet assembles ready to invade

William waiting in France for the wind to change

- The wind changes direction and William's fleet leaves France

- William's fleet lands early in the morning

- Occupies Hastings, prepares for battle

SOURCE 2 The Normans having time to relax

SOURCE 3 The Norman cavalry ready for battle

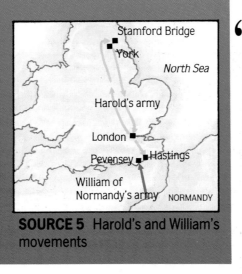

SOURCE 5 Harold's and William's movements

SOURCE 4 Written by William of Malmesbury, 70 years later

Harold, elated by his success at Stamford Bridge, decided to give no part of the spoils to his soldiers. Many left his army as he was proceeding to the Battle of Hastings, so he had very few soldiers with him.

You may already have made up your mind about which side was likely to win the battle, but we need to see what actually happened. Was there any chance that Harold could win?

HAROLD V. WILLIAM: WHO WILL WIN?

SOURCE 6 A scene from the Bayeux Tapestry

What happened in the battle?

SOURCE 7 A Norman account by William of Poitiers. He was not at the battle

> William's army advanced steadily in good order. The crossbowmen were at the front. Next came the infantry, and the knights were at the back.
>
> Harold's army was a vast host, gathered from all the provinces of England and reinforced by their allies the Danes. They did not care to fight on equal terms, so they took up their position on a hill with a forest behind them. They dismounted and drew themselves up in close order on foot.
>
> The Norman foot-soldiers then attacked, but it seemed they would be overwhelmed by the English missiles. Then our knights crashed into the enemy with their shields. The English remained on high ground and kept close order. They were superior in numbers and in the way their spears broke our shields. Thus they pushed our knights down the hill.
>
> William stood out boldly in front of those in flight, and restored their courage. Our men marched up the hill a second time. They realised that they would suffer heavy losses, but then remembered the trick of retreating. They turned round and pretended to flee. Several thousand English quickly gave pursuit. The Normans suddenly turned their horses, surrounded the enemy and cut them down. Twice this trick was used with great success.

1. Look at Source 6. Explain which soldiers are the Normans and which are the English. Read Source 7 – this will help you to decide.
2. Describe in as much detail as you can what is happening. Include:
    - the number of soldiers on each side
    - the number dead
    - how the Normans are armed
    - whether the English are armed in the same way
    - how the English have organised their defence.

SOURCE 8 An English account from the Anglo-Saxon Chronicle

> William took Harold by surprise before his men were ready for battle. The English army had a very small space; and many soldiers, seeing the difficult position, deserted King Harold. Even so, he fought bravely from dawn to dusk, and the enemy's army made little impression on him until, after a great slaughter on both sides, the King fell.

3. In what ways do Sources 7 and 8 differ?
4. Why do you think they give such different accounts?
5. Were there any moments in the battle when Harold could have won?

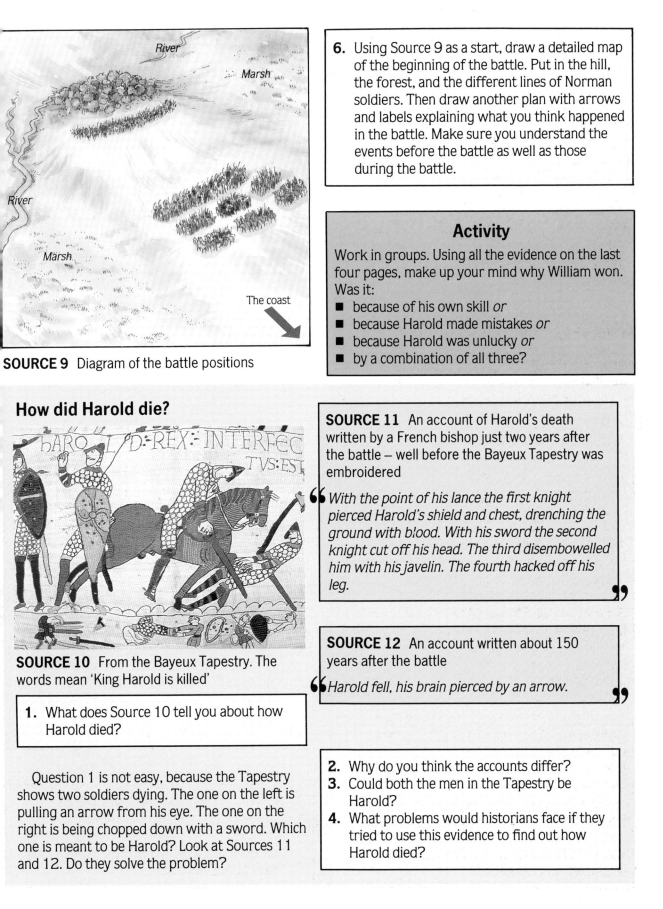

SOURCE 9 Diagram of the battle positions

6. Using Source 9 as a start, draw a detailed map of the beginning of the battle. Put in the hill, the forest, and the different lines of Norman soldiers. Then draw another plan with arrows and labels explaining what you think happened in the battle. Make sure you understand the events before the battle as well as those during the battle.

Activity

Work in groups. Using all the evidence on the last four pages, make up your mind why William won. Was it:

- because of his own skill *or*
- because Harold made mistakes *or*
- because Harold was unlucky *or*
- by a combination of all three?

How did Harold die?

SOURCE 10 From the Bayeux Tapestry. The words mean 'King Harold is killed'

1. What does Source 10 tell you about how Harold died?

Question 1 is not easy, because the Tapestry shows two soldiers dying. The one on the left is pulling an arrow from his eye. The one on the right is being chopped down with a sword. Which one is meant to be Harold? Look at Sources 11 and 12. Do they solve the problem?

SOURCE 11 An account of Harold's death written by a French bishop just two years after the battle – well before the Bayeux Tapestry was embroidered

> *With the point of his lance the first knight pierced Harold's shield and chest, drenching the ground with blood. With his sword the second knight cut off his head. The third disembowelled him with his javelin. The fourth hacked off his leg.*

SOURCE 12 An account written about 150 years after the battle

> *Harold fell, his brain pierced by an arrow.*

2. Why do you think the accounts differ?
3. Could both the men in the Tapestry be Harold?
4. What problems would historians face if they tried to use this evidence to find out how Harold died?

How did William gain control?

PUT yourself in William's place just after the Battle of Hastings. You have defeated Harold. But there is a long way to go before you can say that you have conquered England. So far all you have conquered is a small corner of England. How you deal with the remaining problems will also have an important effect on the English. Will they be worse off or better off?

Some of the problems (shown in Source 1) are short-term. They pose an immediate threat to you and need to be dealt with straight away. But they can be solved by swift and decisive action.

The other problems do not pose an immediate threat. They need thinking about carefully and may take years to deal with.

> **1.** Which of the problems in Source 1 are short-term ones and need to be dealt with immediately?
> **2.** In what order would you deal with them?

Sources 2–6 show how William dealt with the short-term problems.

SOURCE 2 Written by William of Poitiers in around 1071. He fought for William of Normandy

“*Then William marched to Dover, which was held by a large force. The English were stricken with fear and prepared to surrender unconditionally, but our men, greedy for booty, set fire to the castle and the greater part of it was destroyed. The Duke, unwilling that those who had offered to surrender should suffer loss, gave them money for the damage. Having taken possession of the castle, the Duke spent eight days adding new fortifications to it.*”

SOURCE 3 Florence of Worcester describing William's movements before he went to London

“*Earl William was laying waste Sussex, Kent, Hampshire, Surrey, Middlesex and Hertfordshire and ceased not from burning villages and slaughtering the inhabitants. He was then met by the Earls Edwin and Morcar and Londoners of the better sort, who submitted to him.*”

SOURCE 1 Map of England showing some of the problems William faced in 1066

SCOTLAND

> **1.** Many of the English lords do not want to accept you as King. You cannot trust them to keep their parts of the country under control. You need to find a way of keeping the whole country under control.

> **2.** You need to collect taxes, but you do not know how much wealth there is in the country and who owns what.

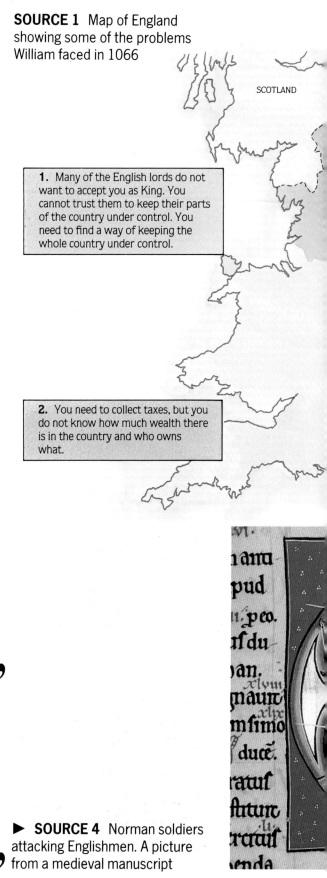

▶ **SOURCE 4** Norman soldiers attacking Englishmen. A picture from a medieval manuscript

5. There is still a threat of invasions from Scandinavia, supported by an English rebellion in the north of England.

ork

4. London is England's capital city. You must take control of it quickly. Some of Harold's troops did not come with him to Hastings. Many of them are still in London.

London

Dover

Hastings

3. There is a very strong castle full of English soldiers at Dover. If things go wrong for you they could cut off your route back to Normandy.

SOURCE 5 Written about 60 years after the events described, by a monk trained in Normandy

❝*The royal forces approached York, only to learn that the Danes had fled. The King ordered his men to repair the castles in the city. He himself continued to comb forests and remote mountainous places, stopping at nothing to hunt out the enemy hidden there. He cut down many in his vengeance; destroyed the lairs of others; harried the land, and burned homes to ashes. Nowhere else had William shown such cruelty. He made no effort to control his fury and punished the innocent with the guilty. In his anger he ordered that all crops, herds and food of every kind should be brought together and burned to ashes, so that the whole region north of the Humber might be stripped of all means of sustenance. As a result of this such a terrible famine fell upon the humble and defenceless people that more than 100,000 Christian folk of both sexes, young and old alike, perished of hunger.*❞

SOURCE 6 Florence of Worcester describing conditions about twenty years after the Conquest

❝*So severe was the famine in most parts of the kingdom, that men were driven to feed on the flesh of horses, dogs, cats and even of human beings.*❞

3. Which of William's problems are Sources 2, 3 and 5 about?
4. Describe in your own words how William dealt with each of these problems.
5. Which problems has William not dealt with?

Activity

a) You are an English earl. Prepare a speech to give to William, complaining about the brutal way he is treating the English.
b) Now write a reply from William to the English earl, explaining why you have to use such methods.

HOW DID WILLIAM GAIN CONTROL?

By the early 1070s William had put down all the rebellions against his rule. He could now think about the long-term problems. How could he make sure that the whole country was under control, and how could he find out what everybody owned so that he could tax them?

The Feudal System

The ownership of land was dramatically changed by William. Many of the English earls died in the great battles of 1066. Others were killed in the later rebellions, or fled abroad. William took land from many of the surviving English landowners. He needed landowners he could depend on:

- to protect the country from invasion
- to keep the English under control
- to collect taxes.

Source 7 shows who held land in England by the end of William's reign.

In theory, all the land in England belonged to the King, but he could not look after it all himself so he granted some of the land to the men who had helped him conquer England. One of these men was his brother, Odo of Bayeux, who was given over 400 estates all round the country.

In return for this land, tenants-in-chief (BARONS) like Odo had to send William KNIGHTS for his army for 40 days a year. This gave William an army of about 4000 men. The diagram in Source 8 shows how this system worked.

Odo had 184 estates in Kent but kept only seven of them. The rest he granted to men who had fought with him at Hastings. These men did not do any of the farming of their lands themselves. They used the PEASANTS who lived on these estates.

---

1. William needed to do the following:
   - reward his followers
   - keep law and order all over the country
   - raise money
   - raise an army.

   Which two of these needs are dealt with by the Feudal System?
   a) Divide your page into four boxes. In two of the four boxes use a drawing with some writing to show how the Feudal System helped solve these two needs.
   b) Which of the four needs did the Feudal System not help solve?

SOURCE 7

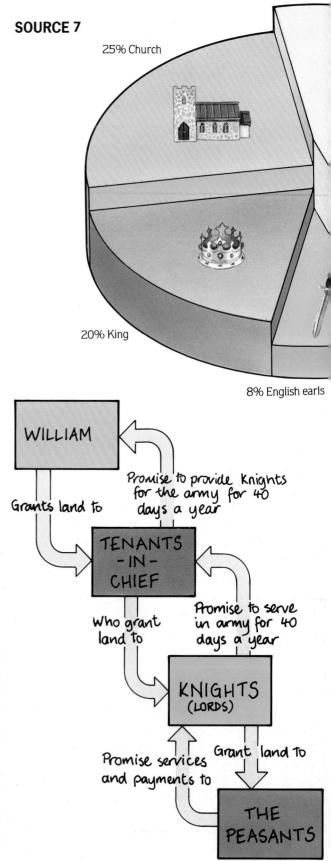

25% Church

20% King

8% English earls

WILLIAM

Grants land to

Promise to provide knights for the army for 40 days a year

TENANTS -IN- CHIEF

Who grant land to

Promise to serve in army for 40 days a year

KNIGHTS (LORDS)

Promise services and payments to

Grant land to

THE PEASANTS

SOURCE 8 How the Feudal System worked

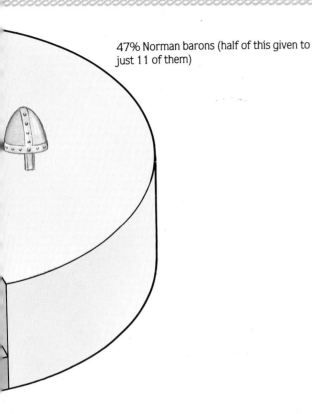

47% Norman barons (half of this given to just 11 of them)

The Domesday Book

In 1085 William had to bring a large army over from Normandy because of a threatened invasion. The invasion never came, but the army had to be paid for. William was already taxing people according to the value of their land. But no one had ever bothered to find out exactly how much everyone owned. There might be some people who were not paying as much tax as they should.

Read Source 9, which explains William's solution.

> **SOURCE 9** From the Ely Inquiry
>
> ❝The King's officials met the priest, the reeve and six men from each village. They inquired what the manor was called, and who held it in the time of King Edward; who holds it now; how many hides there are, how many ploughs, how many villeins, how many cottars; how many slaves, how many freemen; how much woodland, how much meadow; how many mills, what the estate is worth now. And it was also to be noted whether more could be taken from the estate than is now being taken.❞

Remember that this happened only twenty years after the Conquest. Although the survey caused some riots, the officials managed to travel about and get this information from 13,000 villages. A second group followed them, checking everything. It was all finished within a year. Only the far north, Wales, Scotland and some large towns like London were not covered. The results of the survey were written down in the Domesday Book.

You can see the kind of information they recorded in Source 5 on page 24.

1. William used his own officials and not the BARONS to carry out this inquiry. Why was this?
2. Does the success of this inquiry show that William was completely in control of the country?

The sheriffs

Before the time of William, law and order were kept and taxes collected by the SHERIFFS and the shire courts. The sheriffs were appointed by the King. William made the job more important by making the BARONS into sheriffs. The sheriffs paid the King a lump sum, and then kept all the fines they collected. They often taxed the poor too heavily, and even evicted peasants from their homes. The system of law and order became more efficient but it is doubtful whether it was very fair.

1. Look back at the four boxes you made for question 1 on the opposite page. Fill in the two empty boxes to show how William solved his other problems.
2. Which of the following statements does everyone in the class agree are right?
   ■ 'William invaded England in September 1066.'
   ■ 'William had the best claim to the English throne.'
   ■ 'William was a cruel king.'
   ■ 'William gave land to many of his followers.'
3. Which of the statements is there disagreement about?
4. Are the statements everyone agreed about stating facts or opinions?
5. How about the statements people disagreed about? Are they facts or opinions?

Castle building

William was convinced that one of the reasons why he had been able to conquer England was because it had hardly any castles. He had used castles very successfully to control Normandy.

Some English villages or small towns, called *burhs*, were surrounded by large earth ramparts (see Source 10). The local people were expected to defend them in times of danger. But they were nothing like the castles the Normans built (see Sources 11–13).

Source 11 shows a castle that the Normans built at Dinan in Normandy.

SOURCE 10 Wallingford, showing the line of the ramparts

SOURCE 11 Castle of Dinan, from the Bayeux Tapestry

1. Draw an outline picture of Source 11 and label:
   - the different methods being used to attack the castle
   - how the soldiers are defending the castle
   - the drawbridge and the moat
   - the soldier who is surrendering the castle.

SOURCE 13 The 'White Tower' at the Tower of London, the first stone keep built by William

SOURCE 12 Modern drawing of the motte and bailey castle at Pickering

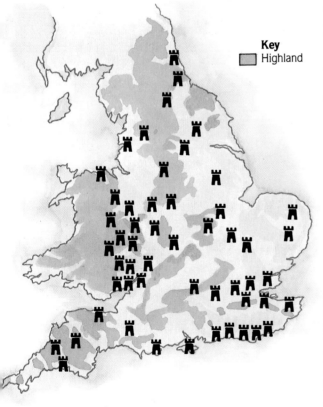

Key
☐ Highland

SOURCE 14 Map showing the castles built in England and Wales by the end of William's reign. In Gloucester 16 houses were destroyed to make way for the new castle, in Cambridge 27, in Lincoln 166

William had castles built all over England. Like the ones in Normandy, they consisted of a motte and a bailey. The motte was a large mound, usually about 50 feet high, and was built at one side of a circular bailey. The whole construction was built from earth and wood and could be finished in a couple of weeks.

A castle provided safety for a baron and his family. At first, barons lived in the bailey and retreated to the motte to escape from danger, but later they lived in stone keeps like the one in Source 13. The castle was also a base for the baron's soldiers to control the surrounding countryside. Anybody wanting to conquer this part of the country would have to capture the castle before they could move on. Law courts were held at the castle, and people paid their taxes there.

2. Look at Source 12. Describe the features which would make it easy to defend.
3. Why do you think the Normans built the first castles of wood?
4. Later in William's reign castles like the one in Source 13 began to be built. What are the advantages of this kind of castle?
5. Using Sources 10–14, describe the stages of the development of castles from the English burh to the Norman stone keep.

How do we reconstruct medieval villages?

NEARLY everybody in the Middle Ages lived in the country. Here and there in the countryside were small clusters of houses with sometimes a hundred, sometimes several hundred people. These villages, with the land around them, were called manors and were held and controlled by a lord or lady of the manor.

What did these villages look like? We are going to look at the evidence left behind, to see if this question can be answered.

The village of Wharram Percy in Yorkshire

The first village we are going to look at, Wharram Percy, no longer exists. Apart from the church, there are no buildings left standing, just fields. But because the land has not been built on by later generations there are many remains for the ARCHAEOLOGISTS to excavate.

Wharram Percy, like some other MEDIEVAL villages, was deserted about 500 years ago. Until the 1940s, almost everyone had forgotten that there was ever a village called Wharram Percy. After the villagers left, the houses fell down and grass grew over the foundations and streets. But over the last 50 years, using evidence such as Sources 1 and 2, archaeologists have not only rediscovered the village but have been able to reconstruct what it was like.

> **SOURCE 1** Evidence noticed by archaeologists
>
> ■ *A parish church stands isolated in the middle of fields.*
> ■ *Three fields close to the church are called 'Water Lane', 'Towngate' and 'Town Street'.*

◀ **SOURCE 2** A photograph of Wharram Percy from the air. Photographs like this were taken for the first time in the 1940s. They can show details of what is just below the surface of the ground

> **1.** Look at Sources 1 and 2. What evidence can you find that there was once a village at Wharram Percy?

When archaeologists visited the area they had to struggle through overgrown footpaths, rotting footbridges and broken stiles. They found grass fields which had not been ploughed for hundreds of years. In these fields they found the stone foundations of rows of rectangular houses. Can you see these in the photograph?

> **2.** Why do you think it took so long for Wharram Percy to be discovered?

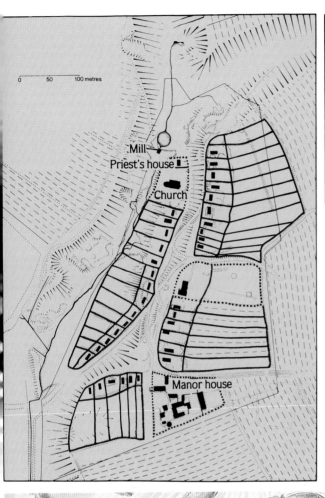

3. Look at Source 3. How do you think the archaeologists were able to put these plans together?
4. Look at Source 4. Describe the village in as much detail as you can.
5. There are some things in Source 4 which could not be worked out from the archaeological evidence. What are they? What kind of evidence do you think was used to find out these details?

◄ **SOURCE 3** The archaeologists were eventually able to produce this plan of Wharram Percy

▼ **SOURCE 4** A reconstruction of what Wharram Percy may have looked like in the Middle Ages

The village of Elton in Cambridgeshire

We are now going to see how written and pictorial evidence can help us find out about medieval villages. Much of the evidence we will use in this section is about the village of Elton. Unlike Wharram Percy, Elton is still a thriving village today. All the medieval buildings were destroyed long ago. Archaeologists have not been able to excavate the ruins. Yet we can still work out what life in Elton was like, even if we can't find out everything we would like to know.

The MANOR of Elton belonged to the Abbot of Abbey Ramsey, who also held 23 other manors. He did not live in Elton and rarely visited it. His officials ran the manor for him. They had to keep law and order in the manor. They also had to keep records of all the money spent or received. As far as the Abbot was concerned, Elton existed just to provide the Abbey with food, materials and money.

The first evidence we have is from the Domesday Book. In the 1080s William I sent his officials to every part of England to find out what everybody owned so that he could tax them properly. This is what the officials wrote about Elton:

SOURCE 5 From the Domesday Book

"In Elton the Abbot of Ramsey had 10 hides of land. There are now 4 ploughs on the demesne. There are 28 villeins having 20 ploughs. There is a church and a priest, and 2 mills with an income of 40s a year. There are 170 acres of meadow."

SOURCE 6 From another royal survey 100 years later

"2 water mills and a fulling mill also belonged to the Abbot, also fishing rights on the river."

SOURCE 8 A peasant's house in a medieval village

SOURCE 7 From the thirteenth-century records of money spent by the lord

"**1286** 6d paid for branches for the barn and the sheepfold.
1297 12d paid for the hiring of one ship for carrying 1200 bundles of rushes from Wytlesmare to Elton.
  12d paid to a carpenter for work on the chapel 12 working days.
  2s paid to a man thatching the barn during 32 days with board.
  1d for a bolt for the door of the little barn.
  6d to a carpenter for making gates before the hall and barn during 6 days.
  2d to a mason for repairing the walls before the great barn.
  5s 2d for 4 men slating the chapel for 3 weeks.
  7d paid to 2 carpenters for $3\frac{1}{2}$ days for repairing the building between the two mills.
  7d paid to a man for thatching the mills."

Most of the evidence is about the buildings around the manor house, which belonged to the lord. Pictures from other villages can help us discover what these buildings in Elton might have looked like.

1. Which of the buildings shown in Sources 8–11 are mentioned in Sources 5–7?

SOURCE 9

SOURCE 10

nostras
Quomodo miseretur pater filiorū
misertus est dominus timentibus
se: quoniam ipse cognouit figmen

SOURCE 11

SOURCE 12 From the fourteenth-century records of money spent by the lord of Elton

> **1307** 15d for a thatcher hired for 20 days to thatch the stable, the dovecote and the sheepfold.
> 4d for a mason to mend the wall between the manor house and the granary.
> **1311** 4d paid for stone bought to mend the foundations of the mills.
> 3s 8d for 38 wooden boards for the wheels of the mills.
> 9d paid to a mason for mending the dairy.
> 8d paid to a mason for making one piece of the wall of the pound.
> 6d paid to a carpenter for making new beams for the kiln.
> **1313** 2d paid to a carpenter for mending the common privy.
> 20d paid to 2 carpenters for erecting and mending the dovecote next to the chapel.
> 6d for a thatcher to thatch the ox-shed.
> **1324** 16d paid to one slater for mending the roof of the manor house, kitchen and bakehouse during 16 days with food.
> **1345** 3s 11d for stones and slates for making a new oven and furnace in the manor.
> **1350** 12d for a mason for repairing the walls of the manor house after the flood.

SOURCE 13 From the records of money paid to the lord of Elton

> **1296** 22d for letting the boat from time to time.
> 3s 4d rent from Adam Bird for an oven, and 8s 4d from Henry the smith for another oven.
> 13s 9d profit from the pound.
> **1307** 6d from Robert the smith for one smithy.
> **1350** 40s rent for the 3 mills, 2 grist and 1 fulling.

SOURCE 14 From cases in the manorial court of Elton

> **1308** Thomas de Chauseye carried away the door posts of the house of Richard son of Ellis, and broke the thatch of his wall. Fine of 6d.

SOURCE 15 A barn

SOURCE 16 A manor house

SOURCE 17 Baking bread in an oven

SOURCE 18 A blacksmith's smithy

1. Use Sources 5–18 to complete this table about the buildings in Elton:

Type of building	What was it made of?	What was it used for?	Where was it?
sheepfold	branches and thatch	keeping the sheep in	near the manor house

2. On your outline map of Elton (which you can get from your teacher), draw in the buildings where you think they would have been. Explain why you have put them in those particular places.
3. You have now used archaeological evidence to find out about Wharram Percy, and documentary evidence to find out about Elton. Which type of evidence was more useful? Give three reasons for your answer.

Living in a medieval village

THE lord of the manor did not farm all the land in Elton. The part which he did farm himself was called the demesne. The rest was farmed by the villagers.

Most of the villagers in Elton in the twelfth century can be divided into two groups – 48 VILLEINS and 22 FREEMEN. The villeins worked on the lord's land. In return they each had land to farm for themselves. The freemen paid rent to the lord to have their own land.

1. Look at the information on this page. What are the main differences between the villein and the freeman?
2. Are there any ways in which they are similar?
3. Would you rather have been a villein or a freeman?

The villeins

They were under the lord's control in many ways.

Services
The villeins had to do services for the lord. They had to do WEEK-WORK every week of the year:
- ploughing the lord's land – one day a week all year
- other jobs such as weeding, hay-making, ditching, repairing the mills, making and mending fences and carting – two days a week for most of the year, but five days a week during the harvest.

Payments
The villeins also had to make payments to the lord in the place of doing certain services for him. Here are some examples.
- wardpenny – 20d a year, paid instead of guard duty
- maltsilver – 10d a year, paid instead of making malt for the lord.

Control
The villeins had to attend the manorial court. If they did not they were fined. They also had to serve on the JURY if chosen.

Villeins needed the lord's permission to live outside the manor. Villeins also needed the lord's permission for their daughters to get married.

When the son or daughter of a villein took over their parents' land they had to pay the lord money.

The villeins and the freemen

There were also a number of services and payments which were made by all the villagers, whether they were freemen or villeins.

Services
BOON-WORK varied according to how much work the lord needed done. Most of it was done by the villeins, but the freemen could be made to do it as well. It usually consisted of:
- ploughing in early winter, spring and summer
- collecting the harvest during August and September
- hay-making. The peasants often worked the whole week until all the hay was in.

Payments
- All the villagers had to use the lord's mills for grinding their corn into flour. They paid for this either with money or by giving the lord some of their corn. If they were caught using a hand-mill of their own they were punished in the manorial court.
- It was a fire risk to bake bread in the villagers' own houses, so the lord built two ovens. These were rented by bakers, who charged the villagers for their services. The smithy was run in the same way.
- Many of the women brewed their own ale (beer), but they could only sell it once it had been tested by the ale tasters and at a price set by the lord.

As we have already seen, the lord of the manor rarely visited Elton. His officials ran the manor for him.

Source 1 shows how the lord's officials were expected to make sure that the villagers carried out all these services.

SOURCE 1 From a thirteenth-century guide for manor officials

The steward
He should instruct the bailiffs who are beneath him. He should visit each of the manors two or three times a year and inquire about rents and services.

The bailiff
Every morning he should examine the corn, meadows and woods. He should see that the ploughs are yoked in the morning so that they may do their proper ploughing every day.

The reeve
The reeve should be chosen by the whole village. He must see that everyone rise in the morning to do their work and that the lands are well ploughed and sown with good clean seed. He should each year with the bailiff work out the services owed in the manor.

SOURCE 2

SOURCE 3 Peasants being supervised by the bailiff

4. Describe what is happening in each of Sources 2–4. For each picture, say whether it is week-work or boon-work and whether it is villeins or freemen or either doing the work.

Activity

You are the Abbot of Ramsey's STEWARD visiting Elton. Draw up a medieval CHARTER for either a villein or a freeman, listing the services and payments which are due to the lord. Design it in the style of a medieval document (see Source 24 on page 45).

SOURCE 4

The peasants' year

Both the men and the women of the medieval village worked hard and carried out very important jobs. Much of the time they worked side by side, but they also had their own separate jobs to do.

Many of the jobs in Source 5 were done by both men and women.

SOURCE 5

All year round
Firewood had to be collected, drainage ditches had to be dug, the animals had to be looked after and the peasant's house had to be repaired.

November
Some of the animals were butchered and the meat was salted and smoked so that it would keep through the winter.

October
The field was sown with winter corn.

August and September
This was harvest time. All the family helped. The men would scythe the crop until they had enough for a sheaf. The women tied up the sheaf. The sheaves could not be left in the field overnight because they would rot. They all had to be carted from the field. Both the scything and the carting were dangerous jobs. The carts were loaded high and a fall meant a broken neck. The carts also had to be driven carefully or they would overturn.

The grain then had to be separated from its stalk and from the husks. This was called winnowing. The grain was stored in the lord's barn or, if it was the peasants' own grain, in the lofts of their houses. The lord provided food and drink and gave all the workers a feast when the harvest had been completed.

January
Much time was spent on work around the house – getting firewood and turfs, planting vegetables in the garden.

February
Ploughing began. Women or children helped to drive the oxen. The soil was sometimes prepared with manure.

March
The seed for the oats and barley had to be sown. A harrow was then used to cover the seeds over with soil. Other jobs included weeding, chasing away birds and ploughing the fallow (empty) field to stop weeds growing.

June
The sheep were sheared and the hay harvest in the meadow began. The hay was cut and then stacked in the barn. The cattle were allowed into the field to eat the stubble.

July
The fallow field was ploughed again. Hemp and flax were gathered in by the women, and laid out to dry ready for spinning.

Remember that as well as all this work on their own land, the VILLEINS had to do their services for the lord. In Elton that meant three days a week of ploughing and other jobs, but five days a week during the harvest. What's more, in extra busy times, such as during winter ploughing, hay-making and harvesting, the lord could make the peasants work for him for even longer.

1. Now study Sources 6–10 and match each one with a month of the year.
2. Which was the busiest time of the year for the medieval peasant: spring, summer, autumn or winter?

◄ SOURCE 6

SOURCE 7

◄ SOURCE 8

▲ SOURCE 9

▲ SOURCE 10

3. Some villeins paid the lord a fine (money) instead of labour services. Why do you think they did this?

Women in the village

Women were allowed to hold land in the village. When a man died, the lord of the manor would normally expect the land to stay with the same family. The man's widow would have the land for as long as she lived and it would then go to the eldest son. But if the widow had no grown-up sons the land could be a problem, as she would not be able to do all the work herself. Source 11 shows one woman's solution.

> **SOURCE 11** From Elton manorial court records
>
> *Agnes, widow of Thomas Bird, surrendered to Thomas all the land she holds on condition that he will provide for her:*
> - *a quarter of wheat six times a year*
> - *five cart-loads of sea coal on 1 November*
> - *a suitable house, 30 feet long and 14 feet wide*
> - *and Thomas will carry out all services owed to the lord.*

1. Which of the statements below do the figures in Source 12 support the most?
   - 'Women only worked at home. They never helped in the fields.'
   - 'Women did not work as hard as men.'
   - 'Women worked at home more than the men did, but they also worked at other kinds of jobs around the village and in the fields.'
2. Which of these statements do the figures show to be untrue?
3. Which of these statements do the figures tell us nothing about?
4. Using the figures in Source 12 and what you already know about the work women did, say whether you agree with this statement or not:
   - 'Women worked in the fields as much as the men, but they did the less dangerous jobs.'
5. Using the sources on pages 30–33 decide what might be particularly dangerous jobs in the fields, at home or in transport.

As we have seen, the women did help with the farming. But they also had many other jobs to do.

Look at Source 12. The figures come from the records of the Coroner's Courts in the fourteenth century. These courts investigated people's deaths. The first graph shows where in the village men and women died. The second shows what the men and women were doing when they died.

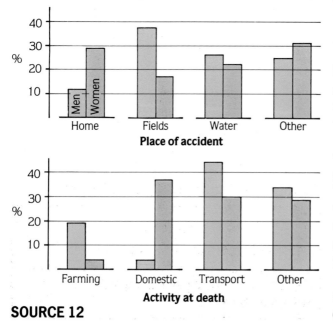

Place of accident

Activity at death

SOURCE 12

The women at work

Before dawn the fire had to be lit. This often meant going out and collecting straw to light the embers. The morning porridge was heated over the fire.

Cleaning the house took little time. The houses were small and the floor was covered in straw. Even though chickens, pigs and other animals wandered in and out of the house, the women still tried to keep their houses clean. Archaeologists have found that many floors were swept so often that the brooms left U-shaped depressions.

Water for cooking, washing and drinking had to be carried from the well to the house. Washing clothes, which was done by hand, was a hard job. Other jobs included cutting wood, baking bread in the lord's ovens and taking grain to the mill.

It was also normal for women to do some farm work every day. The cows had to be milked, the chickens, and usually a pig, had to be looked after. The garden was important as it produced the family's vegetables. When their help was needed in the fields, women hoed, weeded, tied the sheaves and helped with the ploughing. They had to collect firewood, carrying bundles of sticks on their backs.

On top of all this, there were the children to look after. Babies were often wrapped in swaddling clothes. This meant that they could not crawl about.

Older babies were often tied into their cradles. During the busy times, the women had to go and work in the fields or the family would starve. They left their babies at home, or sometimes took them with them. The swaddled babies could be put in trees. Once a child was about five years old it would look after younger children.

Women earned extra money by brewing beer — a very dangerous job, as it involved carrying twelve-gallon vats of hot liquid. Many women spun thread and always took their spindle with them to do some spinning in spare moments. The thread was sometimes made into rough cloth for the family, but more often it was sold to a weaver. Women also earned wages as thatchers and labourers.

1. Now look at Sources 13–15. Which parts of the above description can be supported by this evidence? Does any of this evidence contradict the description?
2. Was the work women did in the village just as important as the work done by the men? Give your reasons.
3. History books written earlier in the twentieth century largely ignored the contribution women made to the medieval village. Books written today have a lot more about women. In the class, discuss why you think this is.

SOURCE 14 Women fetching water

SOURCE 15 Woman taking grain to the mill

SOURCE 13 Woman spinning

Activity

You are either a woman or a man. Write and illustrate a diary for two days in either January or September. Work in pairs. Compare your diary with your partner's.

Field systems

The open field system

THE best land in England for growing crops was in the Midlands. The land was divided into two, three or sometimes four enormous fields. These fields were completely open – they had no fences, walls, ditches or hedges around them (see Source 1).

Each field was divided into furlongs, which were sub-divided into strips. The villagers had strips scattered across all the fields. One villager's strips are shown in red on Source 1.

Between the strips was raised unploughed land.

The peasants had to agree which crop was going to be grown in each of the fields. This was usually fixed by tradition, or in the manorial court.

One of the fields would be left fallow, or empty, to allow the soil to recover. This would be a different field each year (see Source 2).

The village also had meadows, which were fenced. These grew grass for hay. Once the hay had been harvested animals were allowed to graze there.

There was also waste or common land which was used for grazing cattle.

	Year 1	Year 2	Year 3
Field 1	Wheat	Oats	
Field 2	Oats	Fallow	
Field 3	Fallow	Wheat	

SOURCE 2 Diagram to show crop rotation

1. Copy Source 2. Fill in the column for Year 3.

SOURCE 3 From *Piers Plowman*, a poem written in the fourteenth century

If I went to plough I pinched so narrowly that I would steal a foot of land from my neighbour; and if I reaped I would reach into my neighbour's land.

SOURCE 4 From manorial court records of the fourteenth century

To stop people stealing other people's land the Lord of the Manor insists that boundary stones shall be put in to separate people's strips.

Seven tenants are fined 6d each because they have ploughed the pathways between the strips.

SOURCE 1 The open field system

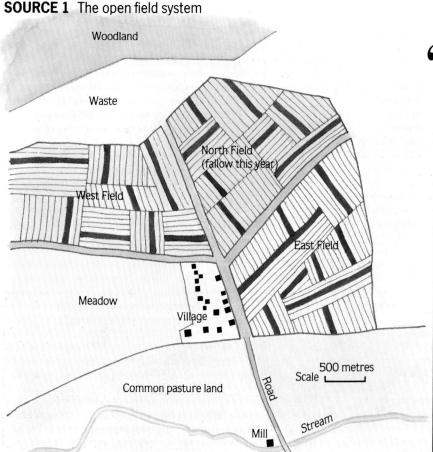

2. The open field system is often described as very wasteful. Can you think of ways in which it did waste time and land?
3. Look at Sources 3 and 4. What other problems did the open field system cause?
4. If the open field system was so wasteful, why was it used?

The infield–outfield system

This system was found in highland areas like Scotland, parts of northern England and Devon and Cornwall. The land was more suitable for keeping animals than for growing crops, and most of the farmer's time was spent looking after the animals.

The infield was the best land, nearest the village (see Source 5). Each villager's strips would be scattered throughout the field. They grew just enough cereal crops to feed their families. The main crop was oats, but different crops were grown in different parts of the field every year.

The infield was used every year and was heavily manured.

Further from the village was the outfield. This was poor quality land and was not manured. It was used to grow crops for a few years but was soon exhausted. It was then used for grazing cattle or for growing grass, while another outfield was created for crops.

Key

▨ Infield–outfield

☐ Open field system

▲ **SOURCE 6** Map showing field systems in most common use in various areas of Britain

▼ **SOURCE 5** The infield–outfield system

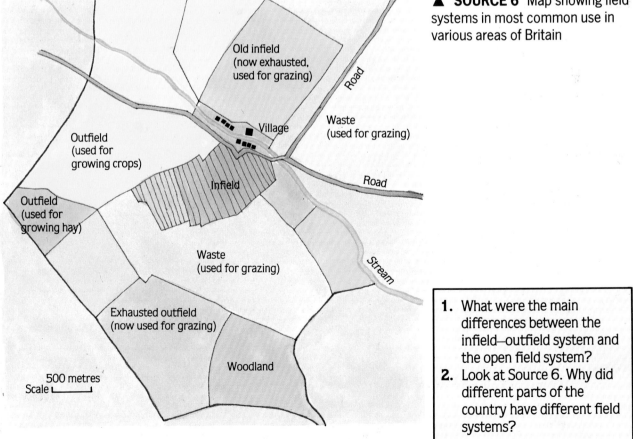

1. What were the main differences between the infield–outfield system and the open field system?
2. Look at Source 6. Why did different parts of the country have different field systems?

The poor and the rich at home

The poor

A GREAT deal of evidence survives about the lives of the wealthy in medieval times. Written sources, pictures, and the homes and belongings of the rich have survived.

With poorer people, however, we need to bear in mind the following:
- Most could not read or write, and the rich did not usually bother to write about them.
- Their houses were made of wood, branches, clay and straw.
- They had few belongings. These were often of poor quality.

---

1. Do you think we have much evidence about the lives of the poor?

Sources 1 and 2 show some of the things historians have worked out about the lives of poor people.

SOURCE 1 An account from a recent history book

Life for the peasants was miserable. They lived in single room hovels with no light. The floors were covered with rushes where the rubbish collected and rotted. In the middle of the hovel was a fire. It must have been very smoky in there, and to make it worse the animals were brought in at night. There was never any time for sport or entertainment and they never ate anything but bread and cheese.

SOURCE 2 A modern drawing of a medieval peasant's house

---

2. List the main things that Sources 1 and 2 agree about.
3. What impression do they give you about the lives of poor people?
4. Compare Sources 1 and 2. Does the written evidence tell you more about the peasants' living conditions than the picture does? Explain your answer.

Sources 3–8 show some of the evidence that has survived about the lives of the poor.

SOURCE 3 From the account book of a fifteenth-century manor, showing food provided by the lord to celebrate their Saint's Day

Beef, four calves, two half sheep, a breast of mutton, a breast of veal, five lambs, six pigs, seven rabbits; eggs, butter, milk and cream; pepper, vinegar, cloves, sugar, dates and honey.

SOURCE 4 Extracts from manorial court records

John Raynald broke into and entered at night the Lord's park where he took 17 oak trees which he used to repair his house.

John Shephard is fined because the clay he took to place on the outside of his walls of his house was taken from the common roadway.

John Yude wants to lease one of the rooms in his house to someone else for a period of one year.

It is ordered that no one must go into the area known as Le Holme and take rushes to place on their roof or their floor.

Four villagers have been fined for carrying away the door of a waste house. This consisted of the wood, a socket stone, iron hanging post, a key, padlock, hinges and a latch.

Alice Kaa broke down the doors and windows and took away lamps and oil.

Philip Hogyns must repair the kitchen in his building.

SOURCE 5 Written by John Gower, a poet who lived in the fourteenth century

Labourers were not able to eat wheat bread; their bread was of beans and coarser corn, and they drank water alone. Cheese and milk were a feast to them.

SOURCE 6 Medieval peasants in their leisure time

SOURCE 7 From Chaucer's poem *The Canterbury Tales*, written in the fourteenth century

*Once, long ago, there dwelt a poor old widow
in a small cottage, by a little meadow.
Sooty her hall, her kitchen dismal,
and there she ate many a slender meal
of milk and brown bread, in which she found no lack.
She had a yard that was enclosed about
by a stockade and a dry ditch without.*

SOURCE 8 From the poem *Piers Plowman* by William Langland, a fourteenth-century priest. He was very critical of the social conditions of the time

*I have no penny to buy pullets,
nor geese nor pigs, but [I have] two green cheeses,
a few curds of cream, a cake of oatmeal,
two loaves of beans and bran, baked for my children;
but I have parsley and pot herbs and plenty of cabbages,
and a cow and a calf.
This is the little we must live on till the Lammas season.
Poor folk in hovels,
charged with children and overcharged by landlords,
what they may save by spinning they spend on rent,
on milk, or on meal to make porridge.*

5. Do Sources 3–8, from the Middle Ages, support what Sources 1 and 2 told you about:
    ■ the homes of the poor
    ■ the diet of the poor?
6. What do Sources 3–8 tell us that Sources 1 and 2 do not?
7. Which two sources may not be much use in showing us how poor people lived for most of the time?

The rich

What was life like for the rich? Source 9 gives us some clues. It is taken from a record of the daily expenses of the household of Eleanor, Countess of Leicester, during a seven-month period in 1265. Eleanor was the wife of the Earl of Leicester, who for several years was the most important baron in the country.

SOURCE 9

❝ ■ *Eleanor received over 50 important visitors, including royal officials, church people and important women. Many visitors brought servants with them. When her husband arrived at their castle in March, hay was needed for 334 horses.*

■ *Much white bread was eaten.*

■ *Large amounts of meat and fish were bought. The meat included oxen, pork, sheep and geese. 'Stockfish' were popular. These were cod without their heads, gutted and dried in the sun. Other fish included 32 conger eels, 500 hake, a porpoise and a whale.*

■ *Dinner was eaten between ten and eleven o'clock in the morning. A light supper was then taken about five o'clock.*

■ *Much beer and wine was drunk. Much of the beer was flavoured with spices. Milk was mainly used for cooking, and water was rarely drunk as it was too polluted.*

■ *Vegetables and fresh fruit were rarely eaten.*

■ *Many eggs were used.*

■ *In the cooking, fish was often salted or smoked, baked or made into pies. Meat was preferred fried. All foods were heavily spiced.*

■ *Most of the lights were candles.*

■ *Eleanor took two baths in seven months.*

■ *Both men and women wore plain tunics. The men wore leg bandages. Shoes were shaped to the foot. Both men and women wore gloves. Women often hid their hair and wore leather leggings in winter. The men often had a beard or moustache. Dyes to colour the clothes were brought from abroad.* ❞

How typical was Eleanor? Sources 10–16 provide further evidence of the lives led by rich people.

Study Sources 10–16.
1. What new information do they give that is not given in Source 9?
2. What information do they give which supports the information in Source 9?
3. What information do they give which disagrees with the information in Source 9?
4. How reliable is Source 9 for finding out how the rich generally lived?

SOURCE 10 Written by Alexander Neckham, who died in 1217

❝ *In the bedchamber let a curtain go around the walls for the avoiding of flies and spiders. On the bed there should be a feather mattress to which a bolster is attached. A quilted pad of striped cloth should cover it, on which a cushion for the head should be placed. Then sheets of muslin, ordinary cotton or at least pure linen should be laid. Next a coverlet with a fur lining of badger, cat or beaver.* ❞

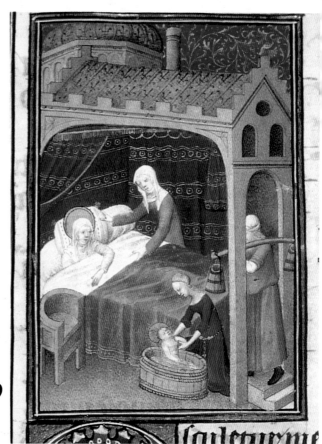

SOURCE 11 Bathing a baby in the Middle Ages

SOURCE 12 A modern drawing of a medieval kitchen scene

SOURCE 13 Sir Geoffrey Luttrell and his family entertaining two Dominican friars

SOURCE 14 Hunting

SOURCE 15 Written by Peter of Blois about the food at the King's court in 1160

"*The beer is horrid to taste and filthy to look at. Meat is sold whether it be fresh or not. The fish one buys is four days old, yet the fact it stinks does not lessen the price. The servants care nothing whatever whether the unlucky guests become ill or die provided they load their master's table with food which is often rotten.*"

SOURCE 16 A fifteenth-century recipe

"*Make a broth by simmering calves' feet and shins in white wine until they are soft. Strain the broth and pour over pork ribs and young chickens. Simmer until the meat is firm and skim off the fat. Add pepper, saffron and vinegar. allow to set and cover with almonds, a few curls of ginger and cloves.*

Chicken should be stuffed with a mix of parsley, suet, mashed boiled egg yolks, pepper, cinnamon, saffron, a little pork and cloves."

Activity

a) In groups, decide what headings would be useful to help you compare the lives of the rich and the poor. For example, one heading might be 'food'.

b) Design a display that compares the lives of the rich and the poor, under the headings you have chosen.

Did people travel much in the Middle Ages?

ONE recent history book said this about the people in the Middle Ages:

SOURCE 1

"The rich travelled most because they could afford it. Also, they had to travel. An important landowner would need to visit his estates to see that they were being properly run by his steward, and he would have important business in London.

The ordinary peasants had no reason for making journeys. Families stayed in the same village for many generations. Their needs were simple, and they could buy most things in their own village. They also needed their lord's permission to leave the manor, and so they stayed in their village all their lives."

We are going to investigate whether the evidence actually agrees or disagrees with this statement. Did peasants really travel as rarely as the writer of Source 1 suggests?

Were there many roads in medieval England?

One way of finding out about medieval roads would be to look for ARCHAEOLOGICAL evidence. But this is not easy (see Source 2).

SOURCE 2 From a recent book on archaeology

"Medieval roads were not carefully laid like Roman roads, with stone and cement, so little is left of them today — just tracks and bridges — and we do not always know which tracks go back to the medieval period. New medieval roads were not constructed, they were just routes which, if used a lot, became tracks."

We can find out about the routes of medieval roads by using maps from the period (Source 3).

▲ **SOURCE 3** The Gough map. Drawn in about 1360, it shows 2940 miles of roads, but only the main carrier routes are shown here. We do not know who drew the map. Some of the routes are on the same lines as the old Roman roads

The third way we can find out about medieval roads is to use documentary evidence. For example, documentary evidence can confirm that the old Roman roads were still used in the Middle Ages.

Documents tell us, for instance, that:
■ Three Roman roads, Watling Street, Ermine Street and Fosse Way, were royal roads under the King's protection.
■ Roads had to be wide enough for two wagons to pass.
■ Anyone attacking travellers on the roads would be fined 100 shillings.
■ Messengers of Richard I rode from Scotland to the south coast using only the Roman roads.

---

1. Why do you think the King's messengers used the old Roman roads?

One document from Titchfield Abbey near Southampton lists all the regular journeys made by the monks to other abbeys in the country. From this document it is possible to construct a map of their journeys, like the one in Source 4.

2. Did the monks use any of the same routes as on Source 3?
3. Why do you think they used them?
4. Why did they sometimes use different routes?

Many other local routes are mentioned in people's letters and in the accounts of traders. From the records of the manor of Elton in Cambridgeshire, we see that regular journeys were made by manor officials to all the places marked on the map in Source 5 to buy things the manor needed.

▲ **SOURCE 4** Journeys by monks from Titchfield Abbey

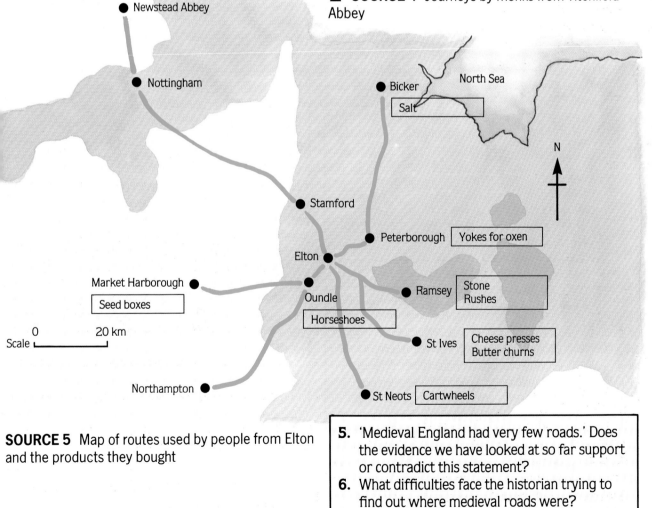

SOURCE 5 Map of routes used by people from Elton and the products they bought

5. 'Medieval England had very few roads.' Does the evidence we have looked at so far support or contradict this statement?
6. What difficulties face the historian trying to find out where medieval roads were?

DID PEOPLE TRAVEL MUCH IN THE MIDDLE AGES?

What problems did travellers face?

As you have seen, there were a few main roads in medieval England. However, there were also many small local tracks joining villages to the local market town, and to other villages.

History books often disagree about what the roads were like, as we can see in Sources 6 and 7.

SOURCE 6

❝The means of communication were fairly good, and the main roads, even in winter, were kept in good condition.❞

SOURCE 7

❝The roads were very bad indeed, because no one mended them. Farmers ploughed some of them, and in bad weather most of the roads became impossible to use.❞

Now let's look at some evidence from the Middle Ages, and see which of the statements in Sources 6 and 7 they support.

SOURCE 8 From fifteenth-century town records

❝At Aylesbury, the local miller dug clay out of the road, creating a pit so large that a glove seller passing through the town fell into it and was drowned. The local jury did not punish the miller because there was nowhere else he could get the clay he needed.❞

SOURCE 9 A description of the roads written in 1406

❝This year has been remarkable for terrible floods and rains. The roads between London and Greenwich were broken. The cartway between Whitney Bridge and Hereford was nearly swept away. In the Isle of Ely, around Cambridge, roads and bridges were wrecked and washed away. The sheriffs sent their men to request money from abbots and landowners, and indulgences were freely offered by the bishops to all who helped in repairing the damage.❞

SOURCE 10 From the records of Parliament. An account of a journey from Northamptonshire to London in 1450

❝160 persons and more, all dressed in the form of war with light helmets, long swords and other weapons, hid under a large hedge next to the highway and lay in wait for William Tresham from midnight to the hour of six, at which time William appeared. They attacked him and smote him through the body and foot and more. He died. And they gave him many more deadly wounds and cut his throat.❞

SOURCE 11 A traveller's description of the roads in 1400

❝Travellers often lose their way and go ways which are unknown. Therefore knots are often made in the branches of trees and bushes to mark the highway.❞

---

1. According to Sources 8–11, what problems did travellers face?
2. Does the evidence so far suggest that roads were in good or bad condition?

A good way of discovering what condition the roads were in is to look at how people tried to improve the roads and make travel easier (see Sources 12–14).

SOURCE 12 In 1285, the King and Parliament passed the Statute of Winchester

❝Highways leading from one market town to another shall be widened where there are bushes or ditches, so that there will be no bushes or ditches for a man to hide to do hurt within 200 feet of the road.❞

Methods of transport

SOURCE 13 From the Records of the Borough of Nottingham, 1370

The King allows the mayors of Nottingham to start a ferry service across the River Trent, on condition that all the profits shall be used on the repairing of the bridge, which has been broken for over 70 years.

SOURCE 14 A letter from King Edward I to the Prior and people of Dunstable in 1285

Because we have learnt that the high roads which stretch through Dunstable are so broken up by the frequent passage of carts, that dangerous injuries threaten those using these roads, we command each one of you according to his means to fill in and mend the roads.

3. Read Sources 12–14. Why do you think a) the King, and b) lords of the manor, wanted to keep the roads in good condition?
4. Do Sources 12–14 prove that the roads were looked after and kept in good condition?
5. Why do you think the historians in Sources 6 and 7 disagree about the condition of medieval roads?

SOURCE 15 Packhorses carrying woolpacks, drawn in the thirteenth century

SOURCE 16 A harvest waggon drawn in the early fourteenth century. Notice the spiked wheels

1. How are these two methods of transporting goods different?
2. Which method do you think is the best?

43

DID PEOPLE TRAVEL MUCH IN THE MIDDLE AGES?

SOURCE 17 River routes in England

SOURCE 18 Unloading grain from a barge. Drawn in the late fifteenth century

1. What would be a) the advantages, and b) the disadvantages, of transporting goods by water?

Activity

You have to transport wool clippings from Carlisle to London (see the map in Source 17). Plan your journey, using the evidence in this section to help you work out:
a) what method of transport you are going to use
b) what places you will travel through
c) what problems you face.
Your teacher will give you an extract from a novel, *The Woolpack*, by Cynthia Harnett.

Why different people travelled

1. Study Sources 19–25. Draw up a table of all the different types of people who travelled. For each person say what their reason for travelling was.

SOURCE 19 Written by the Mayor of Exeter about a business trip to London in 1448

6 *On Wednesday at seven in the morning I rode out of Exeter to London [170 miles]. The next Saturday at seven in the morning I came to London.*

SOURCE 20 A recent account of the journeys of the Lestrange family from their home in Hunstanton to their home in London in the fifteenth century

6 *On their frequent journeys to London, the Lestranges usually halted at Castleacre, Brandon, Newmarket, Babraham, Barkway, Ware and Waltham. Most of these are on or near a river crossing, and they are spaced out at intervals of twelve to eighteen miles. These places were recognised stages where they called for refreshments, beds or fresh horses. They usually stopped at Newmarket the first night, at Ware the second, and reached London after two and a half days' travel.*

SOURCE 21 From a recent book on medieval towns

6 *The area served by a market town was governed by how far someone could walk to and from the town, and do their business, in a day. This was usually about ten miles each way.*
Within that area, the market town had to provide everything people needed which they could not provide themselves.
The small town of Stratford-upon-Avon had the following traders: weavers, fullers, dyers, tanners, shoemakers, glovemakers, tailors, carpenters, tilers, coopers, smiths, locksmiths, millers, a wheelwright, an oil-maker, a rope-maker, a butcher, a dairy, a baker and a cook.

SOURCE 22 From a recent book on the fourteenth century

Many landowners were lords of two or three manors. It was important for them to visit each from time to time if they didn't want to lose the respect of the tenants.

When a great lord moved from one of his houses to another, his servants and family went with him, and so did a great deal of his furniture, his valuables and the fittings of his chapel. Early in the fourteenth century many great lords were moving about every two weeks.

SOURCE 23 One reason why people travelled was to go on PILGRIMAGES. Many people went on pilgrimages to famous SHRINES such as Canterbury. (There is more about this on page 53.) This picture shows pilgrims from Chaucer's poem *The Canterbury Tales*. They included a merchant from Suffolk, a reeve (who was a villein) from Norfolk, and a wife from Bath, as well as a nun and a ploughman

SOURCE 24 Musicians. They travelled all over the country entertaining rich and poor people

omam dominus ipse
e fecit nos † non ipsi nos.
ius † oues pascue eius
tas eius in confessione
i ympms confitemini illi.
omen eius quoniam

SOURCE 25 From fifteenth-century records

In 1484 William Naynow, an Exeter carrier, said he had been travelling between London and Exeter for over 35 years. He carried letters, pewter vessels and money, in fact anything that people wanted to send.

Activity

You are a French person visiting England in the Middle Ages. Using what you have learned from Sources 1–25, write a letter home saying how much English people travel. Remember to explain:
a) whether there were many roads
b) whether only the rich travelled
c) whether people travelled often
d) whether people made long journeys
e) why people travelled
f) whether there is enough evidence to give a definite answer to these questions.

The growth of towns

SOURCE 1 A general account of the typical development of towns during the Middle Ages, from a recent history book

“*Most medieval towns did not exist at the time when the Domesday Book was written. They grew up for several reasons. Some were built near a good site to cross a river or where it was easy to defend against attackers.*

Towns were often established by a lord who wanted the town to grow because he would receive more rents and taxes. Often the towns were planned, with neat street patterns.

Towns often held regular markets and fairs and this attracted merchants and craftsmen. This made the towns prosperous and led to the building of grand buildings, such as merchants' houses and churches. But most of the houses were small and close together and usually built of wood. Fires were frequent.

Eventually, many of the inhabitants of the towns tired of paying taxes to the lord. Many towns bought Charters from the King so that they could run their own affairs. Towns prospered in the fourteenth century but declined in the fifteenth century.”

THE rest of the evidence on these two pages is about the town of Ludlow. As you study it, you will see how far Ludlow fits this general pattern.

Ludlow

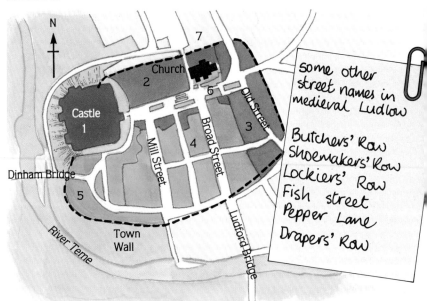

some other street names in medieval Ludlow

Butchers' Row
Shoemakers' Row
Lockiers' Row
Fish street
Pepper Lane
Drapers' Row

SOURCE 2 Plan of Ludlow, showing stages of growth and medieval street names. It was granted a Charter by the King in 1459

SOURCE 3 From a recent guidebook to Ludlow

“*The town's economy was based on wool. In the thirteenth century Ludlow became a major collecting and distributing centre, and had an important cloth industry. The River Teme drops sharply through the gorge west of the town and was the major source of power. At one time there were eleven mills along its length. The Ludlow tradesmen still farmed the open fields outside the town. Their right to use the common land for grazing and brushwood was confirmed in 1221.*”

▼ **SOURCE 4** A seventeenth-century picture of Ludlow Castle. It also shows the church, which was begun in 1199. It is still the largest church in Shropshire

SOURCE 5 From a modern history of Ludlow

No mention is made of Ludlow in Domesday Book. One of William's knights, Walter de Lacy, was given the manor of Stanton (two miles from the present-day Ludlow). Between 1086 and 1094 his son Roger began to build a castle. The site he chose was protected on three sides by cliffs over 100 feet high, commanded the crossing of the River Teme and had extensive views of the surrounding countryside.

A planned settlement grew up under the protection of the castle. The new town was laid out in the twelfth century. The town was laid out with 'burgage plots', which were long narrow strips with a building at one end, stretching back to a small lane at the back. The standard width of these plots was 33 feet.

SOURCE 7 The Bull Inn, built by a wealthy businessman in the fifteenth century

SOURCE 6 Extract from a history of Ludlow

The Guild of Palmers (people who had been on a pilgrimage to the Holy Land) was set up in Ludlow around 1250. By 1550 it owned 241 properties in Ludlow. It had its own street and college. Members paid fees and made gifts, in return for which priests employed by the guild said prayers and masses on their behalf when they were alive and after they were dead. In 1284 the Guild employed three priests. In the fifteenth century the number was over eight.

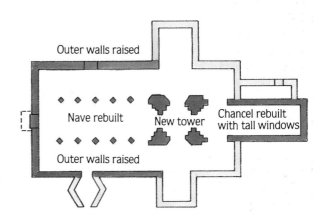

Outer walls raised

Nave rebuilt   New tower   Chancel rebuilt with tall windows

Outer walls raised

SOURCE 8 Plan of changes made to Ludlow Church in the fifteenth century

1. In what ways did Ludlow change during the Middle Ages?
2. Does the evidence support these statements?
   - 'Ludlow grew up where it did because it was a good place to cross the river.'
   - 'Ludlow's development was carefully planned.'
   - 'The local lord was very important in the development of Ludlow.'
   - 'Ludlow did well before 1400 but then fell into decline.'
3. How far does the evidence show that Ludlow's development followed the typical pattern described in Source 1? Your teacher will give you a worksheet to record your ideas.

Market towns

Medieval manors did sometimes produce a surplus (more than they needed). They also needed to buy many things which could not be grown or made in the village.

Look back at Source 9 on page 38. Which of the items used by Eleanor would not have been produced on the manor? The manor needed somewhere to buy and sell goods – a market.

In the Middle Ages you needed the permission of the King to hold a market. But as there was a lot of money to be made from markets lords were very keen to do so, and more and more markets were set up. In Suffolk, for example, there were 12 markets in 1100, but 74 by 1350.

As a market grew, so the town around it usually grew as well. Such towns would often try to become independent of the lord. They did this by getting a CHARTER from the King. This set the townspeople free to run their own affairs.

The town officials would raise money from market tolls paid by tradesmen. In Lincoln, for example, the city fixed the toll so that a trader paid one penny to the city for every horse bought or sold. The more trade that went on in the market, the more money the towns earned from tolls.

Towns used some of their money to pay officials to make sure that prices were fair, that customers were not being cheated, and that anything sold in the market was good quality.

SOURCE 9 From London Court Records, 1327

66*John Bird the baker did skilfully cause a hole to be made upon a table in his bakehouse. And when his neighbours and others, who were wont to bake their bread at his oven, came with their dough, John put the dough on the table. John had a servant sitting in secret beneath the table. The servant carefully opened the hole and bit by bit withdrew some of the dough.*

All those bakers beneath whose tables holes had been found should be put on the pillory, with dough hung from their necks, and those bakers whose tables did not have holes shall be put on the pillory, but without dough round their necks. 99

1. Did all the bakers have holes in their tables?
2. Why do you think the court decided to punish every baker?

Each trade was also controlled by its own GUILD. Source 10 lists the regulations of the Weavers' Guild in Shrewsbury.

SOURCE 10

66*If a member of the guild lived in adultery, none of the other members of the guild were to have anything to do with him.*

No outsiders were allowed to sell cloth within the town.

No member could take more than one apprentice at a time.

A widow of a member could continue the craft of her husband for no longer than three months, when the stock would run out. 99

3. Why do you think the Weavers' Guild made each of these rules?

▶ **SOURCE 11** A medieval shoe shop

Traders began to use the front ground floor of their homes as shops and workshops (see Source 11). The front shutter could fold down into the roadway for use as a counter during opening hours.

▶ **SOURCE 12** A medieval market

▼ **SOURCE 13** A guild master and his apprentices

Conditions in medieval towns

SOURCE 14 From court records, 1321

"*The jury decided that the lane called Ebbegate which runs between the houses of Master John de Pulteneye and Master Thomas at Wytte used to be a right of way until it was closed up by them. They built latrines which project out from the walls of the houses. From these latrines human filth falls on to the heads of the passers by.*"

SOURCE 15 From medieval court records

"*That no one shall have any pig in the town, penalty 4d a pig. Four men are elected to put pigs in the common pinfold.*"

SOURCE 16 Written by a foreign visitor in the early sixteenth century

"*The floors of the houses are of clay, strewed with rushes, under which lies undisturbed an ancient collection of beer, grease, bones, excrements of animals and men.*"

1. Using Sources 1–16, compare life in the town with what you already know of life in the village. Divide into groups. Each group should choose one of the following headings: jobs, standard of living, danger of catching disease, personal freedom.

2. Villeins sometimes went to towns to escape from the control of their lords. Can you see why villagers might prefer life in a town?

3. You are a villein. Write a letter to your family explaining how your life in the town is different to their life in the village.

How religious were people in the Middle Ages

RELIGION played a very important part in every aspect of people's lives in the Middle Ages. It was something which was with them every minute of the day. People thought God and the saints controlled every part of their lives, like illnesses, the weather and good fortune in business.

Every village had a church. It was usually right in the centre of the village. All around the village there would be SHRINES to particular saints, and holy crosses. Everybody had to go to church on Sundays and other holy days. The church also played an essential role in the most important stages in a person's life — with special services for birth, marriage and death.

Even the calendar was shaped by religion. The main feasts in every village were on special holy days, such as Candlemas (2 February), Palm Sunday, Easter and Christmas. Rents were paid on Lady Day (25 March) and Michaelmas (29 September).

Most people could not read the Bible for themselves. One way they learned about the life and teachings of Christ was from the paintings which could be found on the walls of most churches. As the services were carried out in a language (Latin) which they did not understand, all they could do was look at the paintings.

The painting in Source 1 shows a ladder going from Earth, through Hell, and finally reaching Heaven. The souls of dead men and women are trying to climb the ladder to get to Heaven. People were desperate to keep out of Hell, where they would stay in agony for the rest of time!

SOURCE 1 A medieval wall painting from a church in Surrey

How to get to Heaven

To get to Heaven people had to be free of sin. Since most people were committing sins all the time this was very difficult. They had to confess these sins and be genuinely sorry for committing them. This was done in various ways.

The priests

The men who were meant to help the people live good lives and get to Heaven were the PRIESTS. They were meant to be special people, different from everyone else. They were not allowed to marry, as they had to devote their lives to God, and they had special powers like being able to forgive people their sins.

England was divided into about 9000 parishes. In most cases a parish covered the same area as a MANOR. There was a priest in control of every parish.

Sources 2 and 3 are two stories told by priests to show people how they should live.

SOURCE 2

❝I find in the chronicles that there was once a worthy woman who had hated a poor woman for more than seven years. When the worthy woman went to church, the priest told her to forgive her enemy. She said she had forgiven her.

When the church service was over, the neighbours went to her house with presents to cheer her and to thank God. But then the woman said, 'Do you think I forgave her with my heart as I did with my mouth. No!' Then the Devil came down and strangled her there in front of everybody. So make sure that when you make promises you make them with the heart, without any deceit.❞

SOURCE 3

❝A woman lived with a priest and bore him four sons. After the priest died, the sons tried to persuade their mother to ask forgiveness for her deadly sin, but she refused.

The mother died soon after and for three nights the sons sat by her body. On the first night, at midnight, to their terror, the bier began to shake. On the second night it shook again and suddenly a devil appeared, seized the corpse, and dragged it towards the door. The sons fought to win the body back and tied it to the bier to keep it safe. On the third night at midnight a whole host of devils invaded the house and took the body, no one knows where, without end forevermore.❞

1. Here is a list of things happening in Hell. Match these up with the figures in the painting.
   - murderers being put into a pot of boiling water
   - a money lender burning on flames, still counting his gold
   - a bridge of spikes for dishonest tradesmen (can you see which tradesmen are shown?)
   - demons pulling people off the ladder
   - a woman having her hand bitten by a dog. She is confessing to pampering her own dogs with meat when poor people were going hungry
   - a drunken pilgrim drinking from a wine bottle.
2. Here is a list of things happening in Heaven. Match these up with the figures in the painting.
   - Christ defeating the Devil, who has his hands tied
   - St Michael weighing people's goodness to see if they should go to Heaven or Hell. (What do you think the demon on the left is doing?)
   - angels helping people up the ladder.

1. Why do you think priests told stories like these?
2. What do the wall painting and these two stories tell you about people's religious beliefs at that time?
3. How do you think you would have felt if you had been a medieval peasant in church looking at Source 1, and listening to stories like Sources 2 and 3? Would you have been terrified, amused, worried or bored?
4. Do you think this picture was trying to show that it is easy to get to Heaven or very difficult?

The priest was obviously very important to the villagers, but he was not always popular. One reason for this was the payments that the villagers had to make to the priest.

The villagers had to give the priest a tithe (one tenth of everything they produced on their land). So if they harvested ten sheaves of corn they would give the priest one sheaf. Source 4 tells us what the villagers of Foxton in Cambridgeshire tried to do with the sheaves they were paying to the priest:

SOURCE 4 From court records

Ten of the tenants were each fined 2d because they made their sheaves much smaller, when they ought to have made them of the same size as they did when working for the Lady of the Manor.

The priest also received someone's second best working animal when they died, and kept collections made in the church at special services, e.g. at Christmas and Easter.

This extract from Chaucer's *Canterbury Tales* gives us one view of a priest in the Middle Ages.

SOURCE 5

He truly knew Christ's gospel and would preach it devoutly to parishioners . . .
. . . He preferred beyond a doubt
giving to poor parishioners round about
both from church offering and his property;
he could in little find sufficiency.
Wide was his parish, with houses far asunder,
yet he neglected not, in rain or thunder,
in sickness or in grief, to pay a call
on the remotest, whether great or small.
The true example that a priest should give
is one of cleanness, how his sheep should live.
He did not set his parish to hire
and leave his sheep in the mire,
or run to London to earn easy bread.
His business was to show a fair behaviour
and draw men thus to Heaven and their saviour.

---

1. Make a list of all the ways this priest helped his parishioners (the people living in his parish).

SOURCE 6 A medieval drawing of the priest from the *Canterbury Tales*

However, not all parishes were lucky enough to have a priest like Chaucer's. Many priests did not live in their parishes. They often had more than one parish, and as they could not live in all of them they appointed deputies to do their work.

These deputies were often from ordinary village families and poorly educated. They were badly paid by the priest, who kept most of the money for himself. The deputies stumbled through the services, hardly understanding them, and very rarely gave sermons or told stories. They were farmers like the other villagers and looking after their strips of land and their animals took up most of their time.

SOURCE 7 From the records of the Bishop of Hereford in 1397. He took evidence from villagers about the parishes under his control

They say the vicar puts his horses and sheep to pasture in the churchyard.
They say the vicar was away for six weeks and made no arrangements for a substitute.
Sir John (the priest) spends his time in taverns, and there his tongue is loosed to the great scandal of everyone. He is living with a woman, Margaret, and he cannot read or write and so cannot look after his parishioners' souls.

SOURCE 8 Written by Edmund of Eynsham, a holy man and great critic of the Church in the 1190s

The acts of the priests have deeply offended God. Priests are polluted by every kind of sin. They never think of using the money of the church to help the poor, but stuff their own money bags.

2. Read Sources 3, 7 and 8. How is what they say about medieval priests different from what Chaucer says?
3. Sources 3, 7 and 8 all seem to disagree with Chaucer about how good medieval priests were. Try to decide which view might be correct, taking into account the following information about each source:

Source 5: This comes from a poem Chaucer wrote about a group of pilgrims travelling to Canterbury. The priest is one of the pilgrims. Chaucer is not writing about a real priest, but is trying to say what a priest should be like.

Source 3: This comes from a story told by a priest in his sermon. It does tell us something about priests, but do you believe it?

Source 7: This comes from the records the Bishop of Hereford made as he visited parishes. However, he depended on his evidence from the villagers. Can they be trusted in what they say about their priest?

Source 8: This comes from a vision, or a dream, of a holy man who was a great critic of the Church because he regarded it as very corrupt. Can we trust what he says about the priests?

The parish church

The most important thing to do to get to Heaven was to attend the church service called the Mass every Sunday. People also confessed their sins to the priest, and he forgave them. This meant they were free of sin.

Source 9 comes from a medieval instruction book for priests. It lists some of the questions priests should ask during confession.

> **SOURCE 9**
>
> "*Do you believe in Father and Son and Holy Ghost?*
> *Have you done any sorcery to get women to lie with you?*
> *Have you spent Sunday going to the ale house?*
> *Have you been glad in your heart when your neighbour came to harm?*"

Travellers were often worried that they might die on their journey before they had been to a Mass, and so some churches had Morrow Mass. Priests held a Mass at about three o'clock in the morning for merchants and other travellers before they set out on their journey.

Pilgrimages

Another way of showing you were sorry for your sins was to go on a PILGRIMAGE to the SHRINE of a great saint. These saints could help you get to Heaven. You can see in Source 10 some of the most popular places for pilgrimages.

SOURCE 10 The main places of pilgrimage in England and abroad

Walsingham (Shrine of Our Lady of Walsingham, the Virgin Mary)

IRELAND   ENGLAND

Canterbury (Tomb of St Thomas Becket)

FRANCE

Clermont (A spring of healing water rose here)

ITALY

Compostela (Tomb of St James, one of Christ's disciples)

Rome (Home of the Pope, where St Peter and St Paul died)

SPAIN

THE HOLY LAND

Jerusalem (The Church of the Holy Sepulchre, which was near where Christ was crucified and where his body was put)

HOW RELIGIOUS WERE PEOPLE IN THE MIDDLE AGES?

In Chaucer's poem about pilgrims, the Wife of Bath had been to Rome, to Compostela and to Jerusalem three times. Guide books were even written for the travellers, as journeys were long and could be dangerous.

> **SOURCE 11** Royal licences granted to ships' captains to take people on pilgrimages. All these licences were granted in just two months in 1434
>
> *John Widerous, master of the* Christopher *– 80 passengers*
> *Roger Brok, master of the* John *– 60 passengers*
> *John Nicoll, master of the* Cok John *– 50 passengers*
> *Thomas Marshall, master of the* Katherine *– 30 passengers.*

For those who could not afford overseas trips, there were shrines all over England. The most popular were the shrine of Our Lady at Walsingham, where there was a special statue of Mary and the baby Jesus (see Source 12), and the shrine of St Thomas at Canterbury (see page 68).

When a manor official called at the village of Snailwell to collect the rents in the fifteenth century, he found that 'nearly everybody in the village had gone on pilgrimage to Canterbury'.

> **SOURCE 12** An account by a visitor to England in the late fifteenth century
>
> *The Virgin Mary is very famous all over England. You can find hardly anybody in that island who thinks he can do well unless he makes some present to that Lady every year.*

Buying your way to Heaven

If you had enough money you could try to buy your way to Heaven.

One of the pilgrims in Chaucer's *Canterbury Tales* was the Pardoner (see Source 13). He sold pardons, which not only freed people from their sins, but also meant they would go straight to Heaven.

> **SOURCE 13** The description of the Pardoner from Chaucer's *Canterbury Tales*
>
> *He'd sewed a holy relic on his cap;*
> *his wallet lay before him on his lap,*
> *brimful of pardons come from Rome.*
> *In his trunk he had a pillow case*
> *which he claimed was Our Lady's veil.*

People believed that nearly everyone went to Purgatory when they died. This was not quite as awful as Hell. To move from Purgatory to Heaven you had to be sorry for your sins, and get people who were still alive to pray for you.

People often left money for prayers to be said for them after they were dead. Rich people paid for colleges to be set up, where priests did nothing but pray for their soul and perhaps for other dead members of their family. The less well-off paid to join GUILDS, which would arrange for masses for their souls after they died. There were over 100 of these guilds in Northamptonshire alone.

> **SOURCE 14** Extracts from medieval wills
>
> *To the Rood Loft 6s 7d*
> *to the bells 12d*
> *to the torches 12d*
> *I will that 30 masses be said for my soul and all Christian souls after my death.*

Nunneries

Some people in the Middle Ages decided to devote their whole life to God and became monks or nuns. In England there were about 130 nunneries, and many more monasteries. Most of the nunneries were small. Only four had over 30 nuns, and many had less than ten. Although the nunneries were not rich, most nuns came from rich families. For many of these women it was the only alternative to marriage, and some women became nuns after they were widowed. It was very rare for peasant women to go into a nunnery. They were needed so badly in the fields.

The nuns' daily life was a strict one. Source 15 shows the timetable followed by nuns.

"2 a.m. Religious services until dawn, when returned to bed and slept for three hours
6 a.m. Got up; services followed until 12 noon
12 noon until 5 p.m. Working on the farm, e.g. haymaking and digging
5 p.m. until 7 p.m. More services; then straight to bed."

The nuns had three meals a day. In the morning they had bread and ale, and for dinner at midday they had beef, pork or bacon. The Bible was read to them while they ate their dinner. Supper in the evening was usually a light meal of fish. The nuns had to remain silent nearly all the time and communicated by sign language.

1. Look at Source 16. See if you can identify:
   ■ the abbess, holding her staff and a book
   ■ the sacristan who rings the bell
   ■ the cellaress with her keys
   ■ the novice nuns carrying the candles.
2. Why did only rich women become nuns?
3. Do you think the women who became nuns led a better life than those who did not?

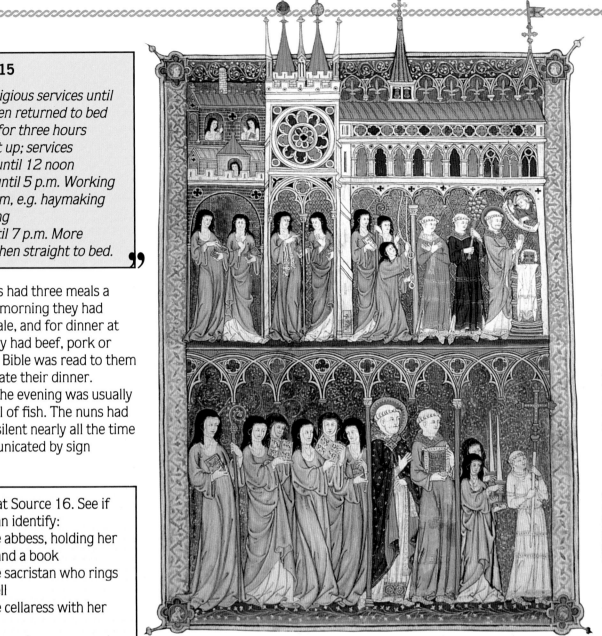

SOURCE 16 Inside a nunnery

Activity

You are a priest giving a sermon to tell your parishioners how to get to Heaven. Using all the evidence on pages 112–116, write down what you are going to say.

1. Sources 9–16 make it clear that the poor and the rich sometimes used different methods to make sure they got to Heaven. Make two lists:
   a) the methods used by both rich and poor
   b) the methods only used by the rich.
2. Look at Sources 1–16. Choose the two sources which show best of all how important religion was to people in the Middle Ages.
3. Explain whether you agree with this statement:
   ■ 'In the Middle Ages, religion was more important to most people than it is today.'

How tolerant were people in the Middle Ages?

The Jews in medieval England

'**W**HY do you treat us like dogs?' This question was put by a Jew to the Abbot of Westminster Abbey in the 1090s.

Jews had settled in England soon after the Norman Conquest. They had helped William raise money for the Conquest.

For the next 200 years they contributed much to English life, including supplying much of the money needed to build cathedrals and fight wars. Jews were forbidden to hold land or enter a trade, but they were allowed to lend money at interest. Christians were not allowed to do this.

Some Jews did very well from their business and at first the Jews were protected by the English kings, who made a lot of money by taxing them. But this protection did not last. There were some terrible massacres of Jews and in 1290 they were thrown out of the country.

As you look at the evidence on this page, see if you can work out why things changed.

> **SOURCE 1** Extracts from the records of Richard of Anestey for 1158
>
> **66** *Easter: Borrowed 60 shillings from Vives the Jew of Cambridge for six months, and paid 24 shillings interest.*
>
> *Whitsun: Borrowed £2 from Deuleeresse the Jew. Kept it two months and paid 5 shillings and 4 pence interest.*
>
> *November: Borrowed £3 10 shillings from Jacob of Newport. Kept it eight months and paid 37 shillings and 4 pence interest.*
>
> *I still owe the money and all the interest.* **99**

> **SOURCE 2** Written by William of Newburgh – a Christian priest – in 1196
>
> **66** *To that treacherous nation and enemy of the Christians, the Jews, King Henry II gave unfair help because of the profits he received from their money lending. He did this to such an extent that they showed themselves insolent towards Christians, and inflicted great injuries upon them.* **99**

> 1. Do Sources 1 and 2 show that at first the Jews did well in England?
> 2. Is there any evidence here that people were beginning to hate the Jews? Explain your answer.

In 1144 a Christian boy called William disappeared. He was found dead in Thorpe Wood near Norwich. Rumours quickly spread that he had been crucified by the Jews. His tomb in Norwich Cathedral became a great attraction for pilgrims. In the following years the Jews were blamed for other unexplained deaths of young boys all over Europe.

SOURCE 3 A medieval engraving. It shows a Christian boy being crucified by Jews

> 3. There was no evidence that any Jews had anything to do with William's death, so why do you think people believed the rumours? Discuss this in the class. Source 4 will help.

> **SOURCE 4** From a recent history book
>
> **66** *The Jews were obviously different from everyone else in England. They spoke a different language and often lived apart from Christians. They did not believe that Christ was the son of God. The Christian religion taught that the Jews had crucified [killed] Christ. In 1189 Richard I was preparing for a Crusade against the Muslims. But why go all the way to the Holy Land when you could kill non-Christians in England?* **99**

Things began to come to a head in 1189 when Richard I was preparing to go on CRUSADE. Sources 5, 6 and 7 – which were all written by medieval writers – describe the terrible violence of 1189–90.

SOURCE 5 Events at King Richard I's coronation in 1189

The leaders of the Jews arrived, against the orders of the King. The King's men seized the Jews, stripped them and flogged them and threw them out. Some they killed. Others they let go half dead.

However, the people of London, hearing this, turned on the Jews of the city and robbed them and killed many of both sexes. They set light to their houses and razed them to ashes.

SOURCE 6 Events in 1190

Throughout England many of those preparing to join the Crusade to Jerusalem decided they would first rise up against the Jews. And so, on 6 February in Norwich, all those Jews found in their homes were slaughtered. On 18 April, Palm Sunday, they say that 57 were massacred at Bury St Edmunds.

In March of 1190 there was a bloody massacre in York (see Source 7). The writer of Source 7 first of all explains that a mob had trapped some Jews in York Castle. The leaders of the mob owed the Jews a lot of money. They gave the Jews a choice: to become Christians, to be massacred, or to kill themselves. This is what happened next.

SOURCE 7 Written by William of Newburgh, a Christian, six years after the events he describes

The Jews burnt their own most precious possessions. Then they prepared their throats for the sacrifice. Joce cut the throats of Anna, his wife, and his sons. All of them died together.

At daybreak, crowds of people stormed the castle. Those Jews who were left threw down the bodies. Many of our men were horrified, but the leaders of the crowd persuaded the remaining Jews to come out. They then butchered them.

Things did not get better for the Jews. In 1253 a law was passed that 'No Christian shall eat with a Jew, and every Jew shall wear on his breast a large badge'.

In the thirteenth century the English kings taxed the Jews so heavily that most of them became poor. Then, in 1290, Edward I threw all the Jews out of the country.

SOURCE 8
An illustration taken from a book about the Jews. It was drawn in 1277

4. What impression is the artist trying to give of the Jews in Source 8?
5. Draw up a timeline between the dates 1066 and 1290. Mark on it the events in the history of the Jews in England described on these two pages.
6. Do you agree that the Jews in England were treated more and more badly as the Middle Ages went on?
7. Why did a) the kings' attitude, and b) the ordinary people's attitude change?

Activity

You are a trader on a visit to Britain in 1290. Write a letter home to your family, explaining how the Jews are treated in medieval Britain.

Could you get justice in the Middle Ages?

MANY history books claim that violent crimes were common in the Middle Ages, that the courts were not fair, especially to the poor, and that punishments were cruel.

In this section we shall be examining whether these claims are true. You should also be looking to see what changes occurred during the Middle Ages.

The manorial court

The lord's manorial court was the court that ordinary people had most contact with. Everybody had a part to play. It was held several times a year, and everybody in the village had to attend or else pay a fine.

The lord's STEWARD was in charge of the court. It usually met in the hall of the manor house, which would become crowded, noisy and very smelly. In warm weather the court met outside.

The court heard two types of cases:
- the lord's business – collecting money from the villagers and making sure they did the work they owed the lord
- sorting out arguments and keeping law and order in the village.

The JURY was made up of twelve villeins, chosen by the whole village. Being on the jury was hard work and not popular, and many people tried to get out of it. One way of avoiding it was to claim that you were a freeman.

The jury collected all the evidence, presented it to the court and then decided whether someone was guilty and how to punish them.

The hue and cry

This made sure everyone helped to track down people who broke the law. For example, if a villager was attacked she would raise the hue and cry. Everybody within earshot had to come to the rescue and help hunt for the guilty person. If the villagers did not help they were all fined!

Tithings

All the men over the age of twelve were placed in groups of ten called tithings. Each member of the tithing had to make sure that the other members did not break the law. If one of them did get into trouble, the others had to make sure he went to court. They often had to promise that they would pay his fine or that he would behave himself in the future. If he did not, all the members of the tithing were fined.

SOURCE 1 A boy stealing cherries

SOURCE 2 A woman beating a man

1. Describe how the ordinary villagers helped to keep law and order.
2. Why do you think everybody was required to help keep law and order?
3. Do you think the system of tithings would work today, e.g. in your school?
4. You are members of a manor court. Reconstruct a meeting to try the two people shown committing crimes in Sources 1 and 2.

SOURCE 3 From Elton manorial court records

a) Maud struck Emma and Emma raised the hue and cry upon her. And the hue and cry was not carried out.

b) John Joce let Peter, a stranger, stay at his house without the lord's permission.

c) Robert's oxen wandered into the lord's land and damaged the barley growing there.

d) Alex, Gilbert and Henry badly beat Reynald.

e) John Lane assaulted Alice his stepmother in her own house and hit her with a stick, breaking her right hand.

f) Allota brewed ale at a penny and sometimes half a penny and sold it before it was tasted by the ale tasters, and sometimes made the ale weak.

g) Henry Godswein refused to work at the second boon-work of the autumn, and he ordered everyone to go home early.

h) Agnes, who is poor, gave birth to a child when she was not married.

i) Nicholas ploughed the lord's land very badly.

j) Hugh dug holes in the road opposite his house.

k) William Bunstede and Emma his wife took the corn of Joan. Joan raised the hue and cry but it was not carried out.

l) Robert owned a dog which ate a foal.

Look at Source 3, which shows crimes from the manorial court in Elton.

1. a) Which of these crimes are to do with the business of the lord of the manor?

b) Which of these crimes are to do with the morals of the villagers?

2. What excuses do you think the accused would have for crimes e), g), i) and j)?

3. Which of these are likely to be still regarded as crimes today?

4. Why do you think those which are no longer crimes were seen as crimes in the Middle Ages?

5. What punishments do you think the people received?

6. When your teacher has told you the punishments, decide which of the following words best describes them: barbaric, fair, or soft. Give reasons for your answer.

More serious cases were not dealt with in the manorial court. Instead, they went to one of the King's courts. As you will see, the methods used gradually changed during the Middle Ages.

Trial by ordeal – God decides

One way of reaching a verdict in the King's courts was to use trial by ordeal. This was a way of asking for God's judgement.

The method usually used for women was ordeal by hot iron. The woman picked up a piece of hot iron. If after three days in bandages the burns on her hand had healed, it was a sign that she was innocent.

For men, the usual method was ordeal by cold water. The water was first blessed by priests:

SOURCE 4

It is said: 'Let this water be to thee now a trial.' The accused is undressed and cast, thumbs and toes tied together, into the water. And it is said: 'O thou water, in the name of God, do not receive this man if he be guilty, but make him swim upon thee.'

If the man floated on the surface he was guilty and had one foot and his right hand chopped off.

1. Would you rather undergo trial by hot iron or trial by cold water?
2. Why were these methods used?

Both ordeal by hot iron and ordeal by cold water were used in England before the Normans arrived. The Normans did, however, introduce a new way of asking for God's judgement: trial by battle. This method was used in 1249 in Hampshire, for some robbers (see Sources 5–8).

SOURCE 5 Written by Matthew Paris, a monk, in the thirteenth century

The suspected persons were arrested but were freed by a jury made up of local men. Many people in the area were involved, and no one would accuse anyone else. The King's advisers told him that robbery was a frequent occurrence throughout England.

COULD YOU GET JUSTICE IN THE MIDDLE AGES?

At last one of the thieves, Walter Bloweberme, admitted his guilt and then became an informer (see Source 6).

SOURCE 6 From Hampshire Court Records of 1249

"Walter accuses Hamo Stare that they were at the house of Edeline Cross at Winchester and there stole clothes and other goods. Hamo had as his share two coats. Walter offers to prove by his body that Hamo was guilty. Hamo comes and denies everything and says that he is willing to defend himself by his body. So it is decided that there be battle between. The battle takes place and Hamo has given in."

SOURCE 7 From Hampshire Court Records of 1249. Walter Bloweberme and Hamo Stare in the trial by battle. Walter is the one on the right. In the background you can see what happened to Hamo after the battle

SOURCE 8 The bill for the equipment for the battle between Walter and Hamo

"Purchase of:
2 shields	13s 4d
2 wooden staves	3s
white leather, felt and linen cloth for tunics	8s 3d
"

SOURCE 9 A medieval account of a different trial by battle

"They were dressed in white leather and had wooden staves with iron heads on the ends. They had neither meat nor drink before the battle and if they needed any drink they had to take their own piss. Jamys lunged at Thomas, breaking his weapon in so doing. Thomas fought on until the officials disarmed him. Then they fought on unarmed. They bit with their teeth so that the leather and their flesh was torn in many places. Jamys grabbed Thomas by the nose with his teeth and put his thumb in his eye. Thomas called for mercy and the judge stopped the fight. Thomas admitted he had wrongly accused Jamys and was hanged."

SOURCE 10 Another drawing of trial by battle

1. Study Source 5. Did trial by battle have any advantages over the jury system?
2. Study Sources 6–10 carefully. Was the result of the battle left entirely for God to decide?
3. How are the two pictures of trial by battle (Sources 7 and 10) different?
4. Which of the two pictures do you think is the more accurate? It will help if you read Sources 6, 8 and 9 again.

By the thirteenth century trial by ordeal was gradually disappearing. The Church was against it, and in 1215 it was abolished. Trial by battle was still used, but not very often. These methods were gradually replaced by trial by jury.

Villein or freeman? The jury decides

SOURCE 11 The King's court

In 1225 Richard, a peasant in the village of Ashill in Norfolk, was seized by Peter de Nereford, the lord of the manor, and forced to pay Peter money. Richard prosecuted Peter in the King's court.

SOURCE 12 From court records

66 **Peter** defended the taking and holding of Richard. He said that Richard was a villein who had not performed his villein services and so he had seized his cattle to make him perform his services.

Richard said that he was a freeman.

The court said to Peter that he should prove Richard to be a villein and to Richard that he should prove himself to be free. The sheriff was ordered to make Richard's relatives and six free and lawful men from the same village come to the court to say what services Richard and his family did for the lord.

Richard brings one of his relatives, Reginald, who says that his mother was the sister of Richard's father, and that he is a freeman. He also brings forward other cousins on his father's side and they all come and say they are freemen.

Peter brings forward Ordgar and Simon Grim, who are both related to Richard on his mother's side and who say they are villeins. And Peter, asked if he has any of Richard's relatives on his father's side, says no because Thurkill, Richard's father, was not born on his estate.

Richard agrees that all those are his relatives on his mother's and are villeins. However, he says that Thurkill his father was a freeman, and he occupied a freeman's holding which his wife, Cristina (Richard's mother), had inherited from her father, who received it from Gore Stiward.

Peter says that Gore held his land as a villein's holding and was a villein. He asks for the court's verdict because Richard agrees that his relatives on his mother's side are villeins, and the holding came to Richard from that side of the family. 99

1. Read Source 12.
a) Who brought the case to the court?
b) Where did the court get the evidence from?
c) Was this a fair way of getting evidence?
d) Why was there no written evidence?
2. Use the evidence in Source 12 to argue that Richard was a freeman.
3. Use the evidence in Source 12 to argue that Richard was a villein.
4. If you were on the jury which argument would you agree with?
5. Is trial by jury a better method than trial by ordeal or battle?

Now that you have studied this section on justice answer the following questions:
1. Were most cases about violent crimes?
2. Were punishments harsh?
3. Which aspects of medieval courts changed, and which stayed the same?

Was the Black Death a disaster?

PEOPLE in medieval England always faced famine and disease, but in the middle of the fourteenth century they had to survive the Black Death. It spread from Asia to Europe and then to England, where nearly half the population died. At that time doctors did not know about germs causing diseases, but they did have their own ideas about the Black Death.

> 1. What does Source 1 tell you about the attitudes of medieval people towards the Black Death?

Some historians think that there were two different plagues at this time:

Bubonic plague

The germ is carried in the bloodstream of rats. The fleas which bite the rats become infected and when they leave the rats for more food they often bite humans and pass on the plague. These fleas multiply in warm weather but die off in cold weather, so bubonic plague does not spread very widely in the winter. Sufferers have a fever and buboes (swellings) in the groin and on the armpit. About 70% of patients die. It takes between four and seven days for them to die. Their blood is usually not infected enough to infect more fleas.

Pneumonic plague

This plague is caught through breathing. It attacks the lungs. Patients cough blood and spray out germs every time they breathe out. It kills everyone infected within two days and is not affected by the weather or climate.

▶ **SOURCE 1** A medieval picture showing the Black Death as a rider on horseback

SOURCE 2 Medieval descriptions of the Plague

66a) *Apostumes and carbuncles on the armpits and the groin. From this, one died in five days.*

b) *Continuous fever and spitting of blood. Men suffer in their lungs and breathing, and whoever has been corrupted cannot live beyond two days or three days.*

c) *The emergence of certain tumours in the groin or armpits, some of which grew as large as a common apple. Black spots appeared on the arm or the thigh.*

d) *Anyone who is infected by it dies, all who see him in his sickness, quickly follow thither.* 99

> 2. Which type of plague does each extract in Source 2 describe? Make sure you give reasons for your answers.
> 3. From what you know about living conditions in villages and towns, do you think diseases like the Plague would have spread very easily?

▶ **SOURCE 3** Map showing the spread of the Plague

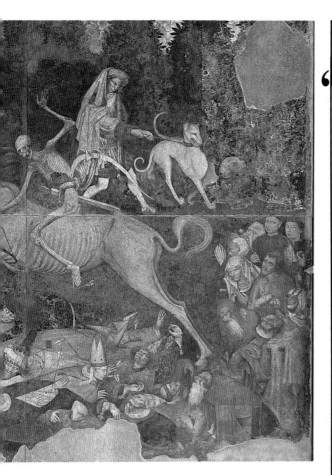

1

2

SOURCE 4 Medieval descriptions of the spread of the Plague

a) *In 1347 twelve galleys entered the harbour of Messina (Sicily). In their bones the sailors bore so virulent a disease that anyone who only spoke to them was seized by a deadly illness.*

b) *In 1348 that memorable mortality happened here in Florence. It was sent upon us by the just anger of God. The city was cleansed of much filth, and sickly persons were banned from entering, but nothing prevented it.*

c) *Jews were burned in Strasbourg in 1349. It was believed that the Jews had caused the plague by poisoning drinking water.*

d) *In 1345, in China and India, fire fell from heaven and stinking smoke, which slew all that were left of men and beasts. By these winds the whole province was infected.*

e) *Flagellants whipped themselves in Germany early in 1349. They believed that the plague was sent by God as a punishment for human sin. They were punishing themselves for these sins.*

f) *1349. To the Lord Mayor of London. Order to cause the human dung and other filth lying in the streets to be removed. The city is so foul with the filth from out of the houses that the air is infected and the city poisoned.*

g) *In June 1348, in Melcombe, in the county of Dorset, two ships came alongside. One of the sailors had brought with him from Gascony the seeds of the terrible pestilence and, through him, the men of that town were the first in England to be infected.*

4. Match each of the extracts in Source 4 with the correct place number on the map in Source 3. An atlas will help you do this. Then write an account entitled 'The spread of the Plague'.

5. Some people at the time thought that the Black Death was caused by bad air. Which of the extracts in Source 4 takes that view?

6. What other beliefs are there in these extracts about causes of the Plague?

7. Use everything you know about medieval people and their beliefs to explain why you think they believed in these causes.

8. Would any of the actions described in Source 4 help to protect people from the Plague?

WAS THE BLACK DEATH A DISASTER?

Did the Black Death change medieval villages?

In the period before the Black Death the population of England rose sharply and there was not enough land for everyone. People were keen to have land, and this meant the lord of the manor would put rents up and increase labour services. Anyone who failed to look after their land was likely to have it taken from them.

Many history books tell the following story about the effects of the Black Death.

> **SOURCE 5**
>
> 66 The Black Death, 1348–1350, killed so many villeins that the lord of the manor could not get enough people to live and work on his estates. Some villages were deserted. In other places many villeins stopped doing their labour services for the lord and paid low rents instead. The villeins became free and their lives improved. Because of the shortage of villeins on their estates the lords had to employ labourers on their estates and pay them high wages. 99

You should by now have a good idea of what medieval villages were like. Study Sources 6–15 and judge for yourself whether villages changed much after the Black Death.

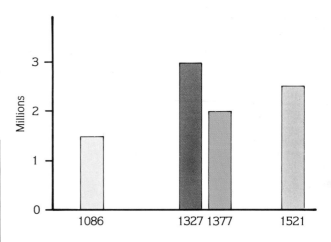

SOURCE 7 Population of England

Sources 8–11 describe some of the immediate effects of the Black Death.

> **SOURCE 8** Written by one of the King's advisers in 1350
>
> 66 The King ordered that reapers and other labourers should not be paid more than they used to receive.
>
> But if anyone wished to hire the labourers he had to pay them what they wanted.
>
> Many small villages were completely deserted; there was not one house left in them, and all those who had lived in them were dead. The lords had to reduce their tenants' rents, and those who received day work from their tenants, as is usual from villeins, had to release them. Land everywhere remained completely uncultivated. 99

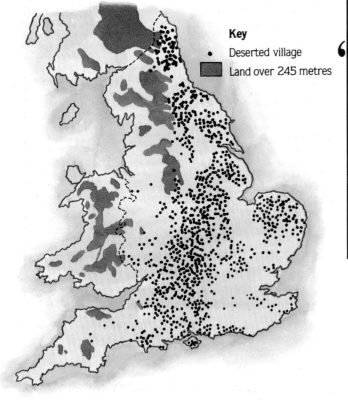

Key

· Deserted village

▓ Land over 245 metres

SOURCE 6 Deserted medieval villages

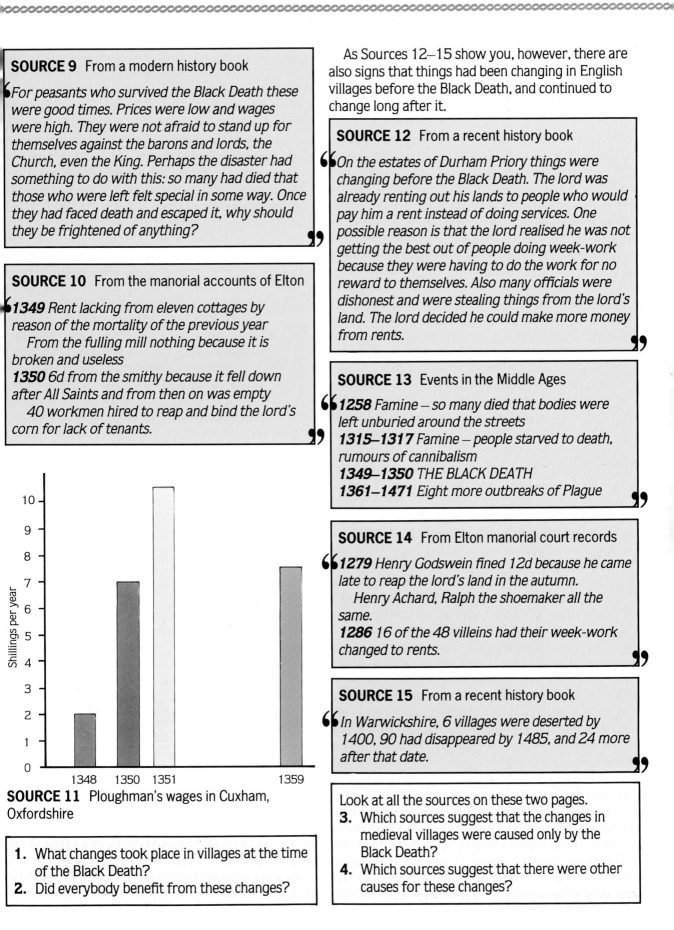

SOURCE 9 From a modern history book

❝For peasants who survived the Black Death these were good times. Prices were low and wages were high. They were not afraid to stand up for themselves against the barons and lords, the Church, even the King. Perhaps the disaster had something to do with this: so many had died that those who were left felt special in some way. Once they had faced death and escaped it, why should they be frightened of anything?❞

SOURCE 10 From the manorial accounts of Elton

❝**1349** Rent lacking from eleven cottages by reason of the mortality of the previous year
From the fulling mill nothing because it is broken and useless
1350 6d from the smithy because it fell down after All Saints and from then on was empty
40 workmen hired to reap and bind the lord's corn for lack of tenants.❞

SOURCE 11 Ploughman's wages in Cuxham, Oxfordshire

Bar chart: Shillings per year (y-axis) vs years 1348, 1350, 1351, 1359 (x-axis). 1348 ≈ 2, 1350 ≈ 7, 1351 ≈ 10.5, 1359 ≈ 7.5

1. What changes took place in villages at the time of the Black Death?
2. Did everybody benefit from these changes?

As Sources 12–15 show you, however, there are also signs that things had been changing in English villages before the Black Death, and continued to change long after it.

SOURCE 12 From a recent history book

❝On the estates of Durham Priory things were changing before the Black Death. The lord was already renting out his lands to people who would pay him a rent instead of doing services. One possible reason is that the lord realised he was not getting the best out of people doing week-work because they were having to do the work for no reward to themselves. Also many officials were dishonest and were stealing things from the lord's land. The lord decided he could make more money from rents.❞

SOURCE 13 Events in the Middle Ages

❝**1258** Famine – so many died that bodies were left unburied around the streets
1315–1317 Famine – people starved to death, rumours of cannibalism
1349–1350 THE BLACK DEATH
1361–1471 Eight more outbreaks of Plague❞

SOURCE 14 From Elton manorial court records

❝**1279** Henry Godswein fined 12d because he came late to reap the lord's land in the autumn.
Henry Achard, Ralph the shoemaker all the same.
1286 16 of the 48 villeins had their week-work changed to rents.❞

SOURCE 15 From a recent history book

❝In Warwickshire, 6 villages were deserted by 1400, 90 had disappeared by 1485, and 24 more after that date.❞

Look at all the sources on these two pages.
3. Which sources suggest that the changes in medieval villages were caused only by the Black Death?
4. Which sources suggest that there were other causes for these changes?

The problems facing medieval kings

The Empire

BY THE time of King Henry II, English kings ruled over an enormous EMPIRE stretching from the border with Scotland to the border with Spain. The vast distances involved made it difficult for English kings to rule this Empire, especially because travel was difficult and slow. Another problem was the threat from neighbouring kings, who were determined to conquer parts of the Empire. For more than 100 years English kings had to fight expensive wars to defend the Empire, until they were left with just the area around Calais.

1. Look at Source 1. How far is it from York to Bordeaux?
2. It was important for the King to visit all parts of the Empire. How long would it take Henry II to travel from York to Bordeaux? (He would be travelling on horseback and covering about 50 km a day at the most.)

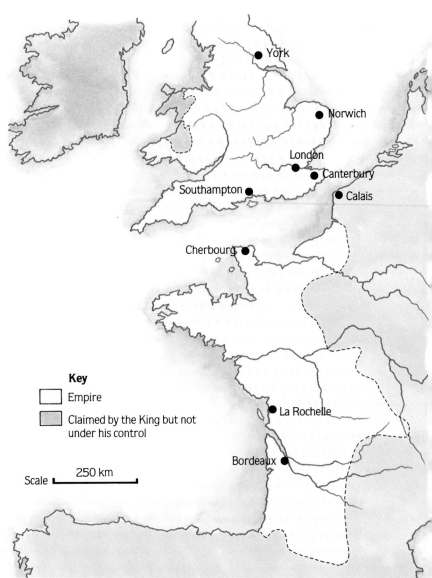

Key

☐ Empire

▨ Claimed by the King but not under his control

Scale ⊢ 250 km ⊣

SOURCE 1 Map of the Angevin Empire in the late twelfth century

The succession to the throne

Today there are rules about who will be the next monarch when a King or Queen dies. Their eldest son or daughter takes over. This has not always been the case. Sometimes the King chose his successor, sometimes he had no children, and sometimes the BARONS wanted to choose the next King. Disputes over who should rule England led to monarchs being murdered and to several civil wars during the Middle Ages.

SOURCE 2 The King dreaming

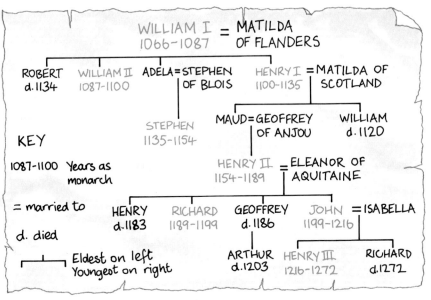

SOURCE 3 Family tree of English kings from 1066 to 1272

Key within the tree:

WILLIAM I = MATILDA
1066-1087   OF FLANDERS

ROBERT   WILLIAM II   ADELA = STEPHEN   HENRY I = MATILDA OF
d. 1134 1087-1100   OF BLOIS   1100-1135 SCOTLAND

STEPHEN
1135-1154

MAUD = GEOFFREY   WILLIAM
       OF ANJOU   d. 1120

HENRY II = ELEANOR OF
1154-1189   AQUITAINE

HENRY   RICHARD   GEOFFREY   JOHN = ISABELLA
d. 1183   1189-1199   d. 1186   1199-1216

ARTHUR   HENRY III   RICHARD
d. 1203   1216-1272   d. 1272

KEY

1087-1100 Years as monarch

= married to

d. died

⊢——⊣ Eldest on left
       Youngest on right

---

1. Look at Source 3. How many children did William I have?
2. If modern ideas about SUCCESSION to the throne had been used, who would have become King after William?
3. In 1135 both Stephen and Henry II claimed the throne. What were their claims?
4. Which King first inherited the throne according to modern ideas?

The barons

English kings could not rule the country properly without the co-operation of the BARONS. These landowners controlled large parts of England, and were powerful enough to demand special privileges from the King.
King John was one of several kings who had to deal with revolts by the barons.

The Church

English kings were not complete masters in their lands for another reason – the Roman Catholic Church. This was under the control of the Pope in Rome. You have already seen how important religion was to everybody at this time. This gave the Church a lot of influence over people. Disputes broke out between the King and the Church over who was more important. The dispute between Henry II and Thomas Becket, the Archbishop of Canterbury, led to Thomas being murdered.

The peasants

As you have seen, the vast majority of people in England were peasants working on the land. Their lives were hard, and famine and starvation were never far away. This meant there was always the danger of uprisings. In 1381 the peasants rose up in a rebellion which almost overthrew King Richard II.

Scotland and Wales

English kings could never really feel secure while the Welsh princes threatened the western borders and the Scottish King threatened the northern borders. Northern England was constantly invaded by Scotland. Various attempts to conquer Wales and Scotland were only partly successful and caused English kings many problems.

1. Look at Source 2. The King is dreaming of problems he faces. Which of his problems are shown in each section of the picture?

Activity

You are a medieval King of England writing to your son. Explain what problems you face in governing the country.

The murder of an Archbishop

1 Becket and Henry are friends

2 Henry appoints his friend Becket as Archbishop of Canterbury

3 Becket and Henry quarrel over who controls the church

4 Becket flees abroad but Henry asks him to come home

5 Becket and Henry quarrel again

YOU have already seen how important the Church was in everybody's lives. You have also seen that the head of the Church was not the King but the Pope in Rome. This meant that disputes broke out between the Pope's BISHOPS and the King about who should control the Church in England. These disputes came to a head in Henry II's reign:

■ Kings often appointed their friends and officials as bishops. These men had no interest in the Church. Often, they kept working for the King's government and neglected their Church duties. For example, they did nothing about PRIESTS who were not doing their jobs properly. Having his men as bishops helped Henry to control the Church in England. The Pope claimed Henry had no right to appoint bishops.

■ The Pope said that the CLERGY should be tried in Church courts rather than in the King's courts. Church courts rarely handed out severe punishments to clergy. Henry wanted everyone to come under the power of his courts. He had a list of over 100 murders committed by churchmen who had escaped the King's courts.

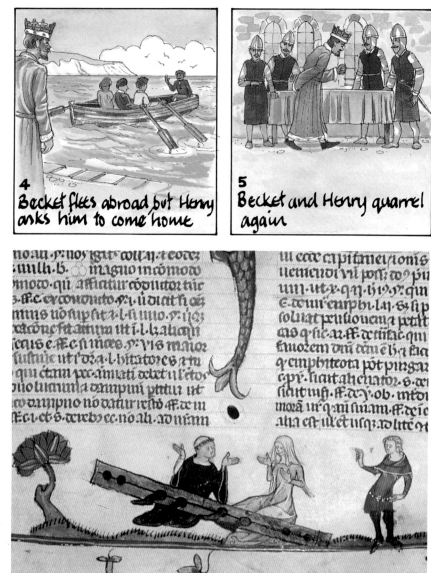

SOURCE 1 When clergy committed crimes they were often given light punishments like a short spell in the stocks

Why did Henry and Becket quarrel?

SOURCE 2 Written in the 1180s by Gerald of Wales, a bishop

Henry was a man of reddish, freckled complexion, with a large round head and grey eyes which glowed fiercely and grew bloodshot in anger.

SOURCE 3 A recent description of Becket

Becket was a vain, obstinate and ambitious man, who sought always to keep himself in the public eye; he was above all a man of extremes, a man who knew no half measures.

In 1162 Henry II made his close friend Thomas Becket Archbishop of Canterbury. Becket was already Chancellor, and for a number of years he had been running the government for Henry. This looked like a clever move by Henry, as it would surely put the Church under his control. But he soon discovered that he had made a mistake, as Sources 4–10 will show you. Very soon, Becket and Henry found themselves arguing.

SOURCE 4 From a recent history book

Becket refused to allow a priest who had killed a man and raped the daughter to be tried in the King's court. He put him in a bishop's prison for protection against the King's men.

SOURCE 5 Written by Becket to the King

It is certain that kings receive their power from the Church. You have not the power to give orders to bishops, nor to drag priests before your courts.

There were attempts to patch up the quarrel, but as Sources 6–8 show you, they were not successful.

SOURCE 6 Written by Henry to Becket

My Lord Archbishop, let us return to our old friendship, and help each other as best we can, forgetting our hatred completely.

SOURCE 7 Written by William of Newburgh, not long after the events he is describing

The Archbishop returned to England with the permission of the King. But unknown to the King he carried with him letters directed against a number of bishops. As soon as he was in England he excommunicated them.

SOURCE 8 What Henry is reported to have said

What miserable traitors I have nourished and promoted in my household, who let their lord be treated with such shameful contempt by a low-born priest.

SOURCE 9 From a nineteenth-century children's history book

Becket wanted to be as great a man as the King, and tried to stop the judges punishing wicked clergy. For this reason there were sad quarrels between the King and Becket.

SOURCE 10 From a twentieth-century children's history book

Henry was a strong King. He tried to force the clergy to obey his rules, and in a fit of temper made some of his knights kill Becket.

1. What kind of men do Henry and Becket seem to be? Do any of these words describe them well: stubborn, weak, unreasonable, bad-tempered, fair, deceitful?
2. Henry and Becket were once great friends. Why did they end up as enemies? Use evidence from Sources 2–8 to support your answer.
3. Look at Sources 9 and 10. Who do the writers blame for the quarrel? Use the evidence on this page to explain why these historians disagree.

How was Becket murdered?

SOURCE 11 This account is by Edward Grim, a priest, who was with Becket at the time of his death

66 *The murderers came in full armour, with swords and axes. The monks cried out to the Archbishop to flee to the church. But he had long since yearned for martyrdom and dreaded that it would be delayed if he fled to the church. But the monks pulled, dragged and pushed him into the church. The four knights followed with rapid strides. The Archbishop ordered the doors of the church to be kept open.*

In a spirit of mad fury the knights called out, 'Where is Thomas Becket, traitor to the King and the country?' At this he quite unafraid came down the steps and answered, 'Here I am, no traitor to the King, but a priest.'

Having said this he stood by a pillar.

'You shall die this instant,' they cried.

They pulled and dragged him violently trying to get him outside the church. But they could not get him away from the pillar. Then he inclined his head as one in prayer and joined his hands together and uplifted them.
The wicked knight leapt suddenly upon him and wounded him in the head.

Next he received a second blow on the head, but still he stood firm.

At the third blow he fell on his knees and elbows, saying in a low voice, 'For the name of Jesus I am ready to die.'

The next blow separated the crown of his head and the blood white with the brain and the brain red with the blood stained the floor.

The fourth knight warded off any who sought to interfere.
A fifth man placed his foot on the neck of the holy priest and scattered the brains and blood about the pavement. 99

SOURCE 12 This account is by William Fitzstephen. He was Becket's clerk and friend

66 *One of the knights struck him with the flat of his sword between the shoulders, saying, 'Fly, you are a dead man.' The knights tried to drag him out of the church. But the monks held him back.*

Edward Grim, one of the monks, putting his arm up, received the first stroke of the sword and was severely wounded. By this same stroke the Archbishop was wounded in the head.

As he knelt down clasping and stretching his hands out to God, a second stroke was dealt him on the head, at which he fell by the altar.

While he lay there Richard Brito struck him with such force that the sword was broken against his head. Four wounds in all did the saintly Archbishop receive.

The whole of the crown of his head was lopped off. But he didn't try to avoid or parry the blows. He accepted death from a desire to be with God.

Hugh of Horsea extracted the blood and brains from the hollow of his head with the point of a sword. 99

SOURCE 13 A painting of Becket's death, made in the thirteenth century

1. How do the accounts of Becket's death in Sources 11 and 12 differ?
2. What evidence is there in their accounts that both these writers were sympathetic to Becket?
3. Does the fact that they are both on Becket's side mean they cannot be trusted?
4. Is there any evidence that Becket wanted to die?
5. How reliable do you think Source 13 is?
6. Which gives you the best idea of what happened, the written accounts or the painting?
7. Who do you think was to blame for Becket's death: Henry, Becket or the knights who killed him? Explain your answer.

Who won?

■ Becket was made a saint in 1173 by the Pope.
■ One year after Becket's death Henry came to Canterbury and was flogged by the monks as a punishment.
■ Pilgrims flocked to Becket's tomb at Canterbury, and still do.
■ The monarch kept the power to appoint bishops.
■ 80 churches and two hospitals were named after Becket.
■ The CLERGY were still tried in Church courts.

1. Some of these results are short-term ones and some are long-term.
   a) Who do you think won in the short term?
   b) Who do you think won in the long term?
   Explain your answers.

King John – an evil King?

IN 1199, 10 years after Henry's death, his son John became King. Most people would agree with the view of King John in Source 1.

Where does this view come from? Most people's view of John has been influenced by J.R. Green's best-selling *Short History of the English People*, published in 1875 (see Source 2).

Green based his account on the medieval chronicles of Roger of Wendover and Matthew Paris (see Sources 3–5). These are almost the only contemporary accounts of John that we have. But both Wendover and Paris were monks — and John treated monks very badly and came into conflict with the Church. They were also both supporters of the BARONS, who fought against John.

Can we trust Source 4? Most of it is very vague: why does Roger not say where it happened? Why are we not told the name of the sheriff? But then at the end Roger claims to know exactly what John said! Government records from this time show that John had ordered that anyone killing a priest should be hung from the nearest oak tree.

Source 5 is another extract from Roger of Wendover's account.

When we check the records, we find that Geoffrey was still alive in 1225 and was appointed Bishop of Ely by John!

> **SOURCE 1** From a recent history book
>
> "John was a thoroughly bad lot. He was cruel and beastly. He made many enemies and killed people with his bare hands. He was the worst king ever to have sat on the English throne.

> **SOURCE 2** Written by J. R. Green
>
> "His punishments were cruel: the starvation of children, the crushing of old men under copes of lead. His court was a brothel where no woman was safe from the royal lust. He scoffed at priests. Foul as it is, Hell itself is defiled by the fouler presence of King John.

> **SOURCE 3** Written by Matthew Paris. He got most of his information from Roger of Wendover
>
> "John was a tyrant, a destroyer, crushing his own people. He lost the duchy of Normandy and many other territories. He hated his wife and she him. He gave orders that her lovers were to be throttled on her bed.

> **SOURCE 4** Written by Roger of Wendover
>
> "The servants of a certain sheriff somewhere in Wales brought to the royal court a robber. He had robbed and murdered a priest. John said, 'He has killed an enemy of mine, let him go.'

> **SOURCE 5** Written by Roger of Wendover
>
> "In 1209, Geoffrey, a priest, said it was not safe for priests to work for the King any longer. John heard of this and, in a fury, had Geoffrey imprisoned in chains, clad in a cope of lead, and starved. He died an agonising death.

1. Study Sources 1–5.
a) Find three opinions in these sources about what kind of man John was.
b) Do the sources contain any facts?
2. Is there evidence in Source 2 that Green did use Roger of Wendover's account?
3. Do you think Roger of Wendover and Matthew Paris can be trusted?

Sources 6–9 give a variety of information about John.

SOURCE 6 From a recent history book

❝John tried hard to be a good king. He visited all parts of England and was merciful to helpless people – the poor, widows and children. But he was untrustworthy and a poor soldier who lost the war with France.❞

SOURCE 7 A medieval picture of John feeding his dogs

SOURCE 8 Written by a contemporary monk who is normally regarded as reliable

❝The King ordered the few monks who remained at Canterbury, the blind and the crippled, to be thrown out, and the monks to be regarded as public enemies.

After John had captured Arthur [his young nephew] and kept him in prison for some time, he became drunk and possessed with the devil and murdered him with his own hand; and tying a heavy stone to the body cast it into a river.❞

SOURCE 9 John's orders to an English city

❝We commit the Jews dwelling in your city to your charge; if anyone attempts to harm them always protect and assist them.❞

4. Study Source 7. Does John look evil?
5. Study Sources 6, 8 and 9. Which gives the most balanced account of John?
6. Why do you think people have been so ready to believe that John was an evil King?
7. Is it possible to prove whether or not John was an evil King?

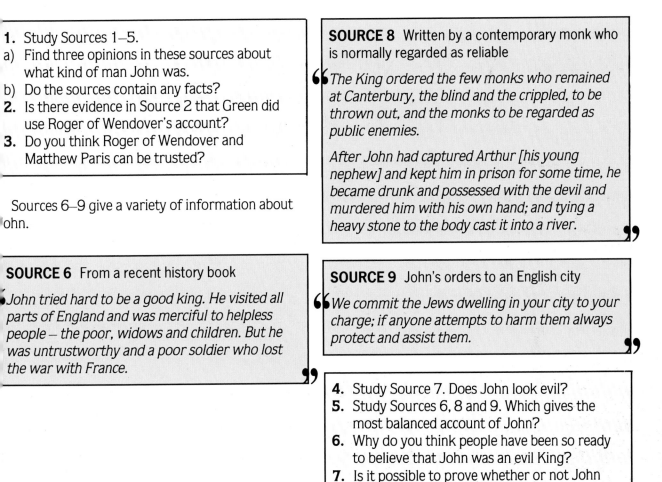

Was the Magna Carta a failure?

JOHN had become King of England at a very difficult time.

His brother, King Richard, had spent nearly all his reign fighting the CRUSADES and had neglected England. He had also left John with no money.

John's nephew Arthur also claimed the throne. Some historians believe John murdered him (see Source 8 on the previous page).

To add to John's problems, there was also a powerful new King of France, who was planning to conquer England's French lands. By 1206 John had lost most of the lands in France. He tried to win them back in 1214 but was unsuccessful.

To fight these wars he had to tax the BARONS heavily, even though many of them had lost their lands in France as well. John also increased the many FEUDAL payments from the barons. For example, it was normal for a baron to pay the King about £100 when he inherited his father's lands, but John charged as much as £600. The barons also resented the payment called scutage. Normally they paid this to the King instead of sending him knights for his army. John turned it into a tax which they paid every year.

John also ran into trouble with the Church. He quarrelled with the Pope about who should be the new Archbishop of Canterbury. The Pope closed all the churches in England for the rest of John's reign.

There were no marriages and no one could be buried in holy ground. In return John seized the lands of a number of monasteries.

John's reign was not all failure:
- He had victories against the Welsh and the Scots. One contemporary writer said, 'Ireland, Scotland and Wales all bowed to his nod.'
- He successfully reformed and strengthened the English navy.
- He made sure his law courts brought law and order and justice to everyone (he often delayed trials to make sure he could be present).
- He introduced a new money system, which helped government finances.

However, by 1215 the barons had had enough and they rebelled. This was nothing unusual. Every King since William I had faced barons' revolts.

---

1. Give three reasons why the barons rebelled in 1215.

In 1215 the barons forced John to sign the Magna Carta (the Great CHARTER).

SOURCE 1 A nineteenth-century picture of John signing the Magna Carta, now hanging in the Houses of Parliament

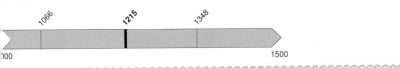

2. What impression does Source 1 give you of John?

3. Look at the points from the Charter in Source 2. Which group of people would benefit from each of these points? Which group of people would be no better off?

The Magna Carta is often seen as the document that laid down for the first time the rights and freedoms of the English people and made sure that we still have these freedoms today. See what you think.

When the barons put this Charter together their aims were:
- to stop their civil war with the King
- to stop John taking too much money from them
- to make sure they received a fair trial from John's courts.

In other words, they were looking after themselves. They were not trying to set down the rights of all English people. They included the rights of other groups, like MERCHANTS and the Church, but only to win as much support as possible.

Much of the Charter was concerned with the rights of the barons – but there were only just over 100 barons. The rights in the Charter were restricted to FREEMEN – but most people at that time were not free, they were VILLEINS.

John only signed the Charter to gain some time and stop the barons rebelling. He had no intention of keeping to it. Only months later, fighting broke out again between the barons and the King, so the Charter could be said to be a failure.

However, it was in the centuries after John's reign that the Charter became more important. The kings after John did give the barons the rights laid down in the Charter. What's more, after the Black Death, as more and more villeins became free, the rights in the Charter also applied to them. Most people, not just the barons, began to pay regular taxes, and so their permission was needed before taxes could be set by the King.

Two of the points in the Charter are still very important to everybody in Britain today:
- We cannot be punished without a fair trial.
- We cannot be taxed without our representatives (Members of Parliament) agreeing.

SOURCE 2 Some of the main points in the Magna Carta

a) We grant to all freemen all the liberties written below.
b) A baron's heir shall inherit his lands on payment of £100 to the King.
c) No scutage [tax] shall be imposed on the barons except with the common counsel of the realm.
d) To obtain the common counsel of the realm we will summon bishops, earls and barons.
e) No freemen shall be arrested or imprisoned without a proper trial and according to the law of the land.
f) The English Church shall be free to make its own appointments.
g) All merchants shall have safety, in staying and travelling in England, for buying and selling goods free from evil tolls.

SOURCE 3 Written by a twentieth-century historian

The Magna Carta made it clear that the King was subject to laws which would protect the rights of the people. It was an immediate success.

SOURCE 4 A seventeenth-century revolutionary describes the Magna Carta's results

The clergy and gentry have got their freedom, but the common people are still slaves.

4. Which of Sources 3 and 4 do you agree with?
5. Why do you think the writer of Source 4 claims the Magna Carta was a failure?
6. Why could the Charter be said to be a long-term success?

Why did Parliament develop?

Stage 1:

The barons give the King advice when he asks for it

IF KINGS were sensible, they ruled the country with the advice of their most powerful subjects, the barons and BISHOPS. These men controlled large parts of the country. If the King wanted to stay in power, raise armies, keep law and order and collect taxes, he needed the support of these men. Several kings in the Middle Ages lost their thrones because they lost the support of their barons, and the barons rebelled against them.

Saxon kings had realised that they needed to consult the bishops and nobles. They took advice from a group of bishops and nobles called the Witan, which is shown in Source 1.

William I (1066–1087) continued this system. His tenants-in-chief (the barons he had given land to) formed his Great Council. Kings held these meetings because they were sensible. The barons did not have a right to be there. If a king wanted to risk it, he could govern without the barons, or he could invite some barons to meetings but not invite others.

SOURCE 1 The Anglo-Saxon Witan

▶ **SOURCE 2** Parliament in Edward I's reign (1272–1307)

SOURCE 3 The modern Parliament

Stage 2:

Kings have to meet with the barons

You have already seen that in King John's reign there was an important development. The barons forced John to sign the Magna Carta in 1215. Look back at Source 2 on the previous page. Points c) and d) mean that the King needed the barons' permission before he could set a tax. In other words, the King now *had* to call meetings of his barons.

76

John did not do this (and we have already seen the trouble he got into as a result). But the kings who followed him did. This gave the barons more power. If the King asked them for taxes, they could demand things in return.

Stage 3:
The Commons are sometimes invited

You have probably noticed that the most important difference between the Great Council and the Parliament we have today is that only bishops and barons were invited to the Great Council.

This changed after 1264, when the barons rebelled again and defeated and captured King Henry III. The barons were led by Simon de Montfort, who ruled the country for a time. Simon did not have the support of all the barons, so to try and get more people on his side he called a Parliament which included not just the nobles but also some of the ordinary people. Two KNIGHTS from each county and two representatives from each of the large towns were chosen by rich property owners.

Henry's supporters defeated and killed Simon at the battle of Evesham in 1265, but from this time Parliaments often contained representatives of the ordinary people, or Commons, as well as lords and bishops.

Stage 4:
The Commons become more powerful

For much of the time between 1337 and 1453 England was at war with France. This was known as the Hundred Years' War. As you can imagine, 100 years of war was very expensive. The only way to pay for the war was to tax everybody in the country. But before the kings could tax anybody, representatives from the counties and the towns had to come to Parliament and agree to the taxes.

The Lords and the Commons met in two separate groups. Before they would agree to any taxes, the Commons began to ask the King for reforms. Sometimes these were about local matters, like the right to build a new bridge, but sometimes the Commons had views on how the country should be governed.

However, this was still a long way from Parliament as we know it. Kings still tried to stop the Commons from discussing important matters like foreign policy. It is also important to remember that Parliament only met for a few weeks every year. For most of the time the King ruled with the help of his advisers from the Lords.

1. Look at Sources 1–3. What are the main differences between these three Parliaments?
2. Draw a timeline from 1066 to 1500, and mark on it the important developments in the history of Parliament.
3. Here are a number of reasons that caused Parliament to develop at various stages:
   ■ the Kings' need to keep the barons on their side
   ■ the rebellion by the barons against John
   ■ the rebellion led by Simon de Montfort
   ■ Simon de Montfort's need to get as much support as possible from ordinary people
   ■ the need to pay for the Hundred Years' War against France.
   Discuss in the class how each of these reasons helped the development of Parliament.
4. Which of these reasons was the most important? Why?
5. For each statement below, say whether it describes:
   a) Parliament in the thirteenth century
   b) Parliament today
   c) Parliament at both times.
      ■ 'Parliament meets for a few weeks every year. The monarch rules the country with the Council for the rest of the time.'
      ■ 'Parliament consists of Lords and Commons.'
      ■ 'The Commons are elected by people around the country.'
      ■ 'Only the rich are allowed to vote.'
      ■ 'Parliament is not allowed to discuss certain subjects, like foreign policy.'
      ■ 'The House of Lords is more important than the House of Commons.'
      ■ 'Parliament has to agree before people can be taxed.'
      ■ 'The Prime Minister comes from the House of Commons and is more powerful than the King or Queen.'

The Peasants' Revolt

What happened?

SOURCE 1 Written by a monk in York in 1399

"At Brampton in Essex, Thomas Brampton demanded a new payment of taxes from the people, who said they would not pay a penny more. Thomas ordered the men to be arrested. Then the commons said they had already paid the tax, and rose up against him and tried to kill Thomas. They then went from place to place to stir up other folk.

And at this moment [30 May 1381] a tax collector was sent to Kent, but he was turned back by the commons. And after this the commons of Kent gathered together in great numbers without a head or chieftain and on the Friday [4 June] came to Dartford. On the next Friday they came to Rochester. They then took their way to Maidstone, where they made Wat Tyler their chief. And on the Monday next they came to Canterbury. After cutting off the heads of three traitors, they took 500 men of the town with them to London, but left the rest to guard the town.

At this time the commons had as their adviser an evil priest named Sir John Ball. A fit reward he got later, when he was hung, drawn and quartered. The commons went to many places and gathered 60,000 men. On their way to London they burned the manors of the Duke of Lancaster to the ground, because they hated him. When the King [Richard II] heard of these doings, he sent his messengers to them, asking why they were doing this. And they answered that they had risen to rescue him from traitors. The King agreed to meet them at Blackheath the next day.

The commons of Kent came to Blackheath and the commons of Essex came to the other side of the water. The King was on his way, but turned back when his advisers warned him not to trust the commons. The commons sent a message asking for the heads of the Duke of Lancaster and the other fifteen lords who ran the government. The commons of Kent came to Southwark, and at

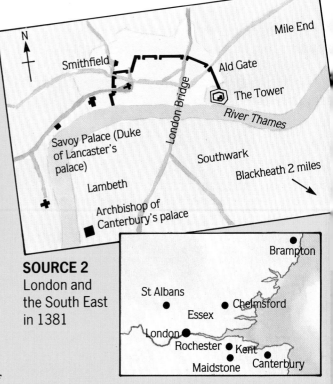

SOURCE 2 London and the South East in 1381

the same time the commons of Essex came to Lambeth, where they ransacked the buildings of the Archbishop of Canterbury.

The commons of Kent went on to London Bridge to pass into the city. The commons of Southwark rose with them, and forced the guards to lower the drawbridge. The commons from Essex entered through Ald Gate. They came at the Duke of Lancaster's palace, broke open the gates and burnt all the buildings within the gates.

The next day the commons from Kent and Essex met the King at Mile End. They asked that no men should be villeins. The King proclaimed that they should be free and pardoned them. The commons from Essex went home, but Wat Tyler with some men then made their way to the Tower, where they cut the Archbishop's head off and paraded it through the streets, on wooden poles. That night they murdered some 140 people, and there were hideous cries and horrible tumult all through the night.

The King told all the commons to meet him at Smithfield the next day."

---

1. Using your own copy of the map (Source 2), plot the movements of the rebels with dates.
2. Write your own account of the main events in no more than 100 words.
3. Do you think the account in Source 1 is fair, or is it biased?

Why did the peasants revolt?

WE HAVE seen that, because of the Black Death, lords did not have enough people to work their land. This meant wages went up, and in some places PEASANTS were able to pay money instead of doing labour services. It seems that the peasants were better off than they had ever been. Why did the peasants of England rebel in 1381? Sources 3–8 will give you some clues.

SOURCE 3 A government decree in the 1350s

Because a large number of people, especially labourers and servants, have lately died of Plague, many refuse to work unless they are paid excessive wages. Therefore every man and woman, free or villein, not already working, shall be bound to serve him who shall require their labour, and receive only the wages traditionally paid. And if any workman in a man's service leaves the service without permission, he shall be imprisoned.

SOURCE 4 A sermon by the peasants' leader, John Ball

The rich have wines, spices, and fine bread, while we have only rye and water. It is by our labour that they can live so well. We are called slaves, and if we do not perform our services we are beaten. Let us go to the King, he is young, and from him we may receive a favourable answer.

SOURCE 5 From a recent history book

The spark that ignited the flames was a check by government officials on who had not paid the Poll Tax of 1380 (12d a head). This tax had to be paid by everyone. This was the third such tax in three years. Those who did not pay were imprisoned. The tax was needed to pay for the war against France, but was seen as an attempt by the rich to make the labouring classes pay more as they had been better off since the Black Death.

SOURCE 6 Written by Sir John Froissart, who lived at the time of the Peasants' Revolt, but did not see what happened. He once worked for the royal family

The lower orders are bound by law to plough the lands of the gentry, to harvest their grain, to thrash and winnow it. In the counties of Kent, Essex, Sussex and Bedford these services are more oppressive than in other parts of the kingdom.

SOURCE 7 From a recent history book

The peasants knew who they blamed for bad government:
- *John of Gaunt (the King's uncle)*
- *the Chancellor, Archbishop Sudbury*
- *the Treasurer, Sir Robert Hales*
and they later executed the last two.

SOURCE 8 John Ball talking to the peasants

1. Events like the Peasants' Revolt usually have many different causes. Use evidence from Sources 3–8 to explain how each of the following helped cause the Peasants' Revolt:
   - money
   - hatred of particular people
   - causes beyond anyone's control
   - desire for freedom and equality.
2. Which of these do you think is most important? Give reasons for your answer.

Death at Smithfield – you be Richard's judge

SOURCE 9 A version of events in June 1381

PEASANTS BETRAYED!

London, 15 June 1381

Today King Richard proved what a coward and trickster he is. Hiding behind bodyguards, Richard played his treacherous part in the bloody murder of peasant leader Wat Tyler. Tyler agreed to the meeting because he believed the King was going to help put right the evils which made life a misery for so many ordinary people. But Richard went back on all the promises he had made to help the people.

In good faith Wat rode across to speak with the King, but was immediately surrounded by soldiers. Out of sight of the peasants, the bloodthirsty Mayor of London hacked down Tyler as he spat out some of the drink he had been given. It is not clear whether the drink had been tampered with.

The King rode up to the peasants. He told them to follow him, and he would see they got home safely, but they soon found themselves surrounded by soldiers.

SOURCE 10 A version of events in June 1381

BRAVE KING BEATS REBELS!

London, 15 June 1381

Today saw great celebrations after brave fourteen-year-old King Richard led his men to a brilliant victory over the peasant rebels who had brought death and destruction to the city.

With courage and majesty, the King rode to Smithfield with his trusted followers to meet an army of 20,000 angry rebels. Tyler advanced to the King, dagger in hand, and spat at him. He then stabbed the Mayor of London in the stomach. The Mayor bravely struck back with his sword and Tyler fell to the ground, screaming for revenge. King Richard calmly strode forward to the peasants and ordered them to obey him. Surprised, they followed him to nearby fields, where they surrendered. The King then let them go home safely.

SOURCE 11 This picture was painted about 60 years after the revolt. It shows Richard twice. On the left hand side he is raising his hand as Wat Tyler is struck down. On the right he is speaking with the rebels

On 15 June, one day after the King's meeting with the rebels at Mile End, he agreed to meet them again at Smithfield. He had already agreed to many of their demands.

Sources 9 and 10 are two very different versions of how Richard and his advisers behaved at this meeting.

1. Read Sources 9 and 10, the two newspaper accounts of events at Smithfield.
a) What do they agree about?
b) What do they disagree about?

SOURCE 12 Written by Sir John Froissart

Tyler still kept up the conversation with the Mayor. The Mayor replied, 'I will not live a day unless you pay for your insolence.' Upon saying which, he drew his sword and struck Tyler such a blow on the head as felled him. As soon as the rebel was down, he was surrounded on all sides so his own men might not see him.

SOURCE 13 Written by a monk in York in 1399

The commons were arrayed in battle formation in great numbers. Tyler dismounted, carrying his dagger. He called for some water and rinsed his mouth in a very rude disgusting fashion in front of the King.

Tyler then made to strike the King's valet with his dagger. The Mayor of London tried to arrest him, and because of this Wat stabbed the Mayor with his dagger in the stomach. But the Mayor, as it pleased God, was wearing armour, and drew his cutlass and gave Wat a deep cut on the neck, and then a great cut on the head.

SOURCE 14 Written by a monk in York in 1399

The King and important men in the city met with Sir Robert Knolles [an army commander] about how they could get rid of the rebels.

SOURCE 15 From a recent history book

The King's advisers knew that the death of a rebel leader in France had stopped a revolt in 1358.

SOURCE 16 King Richard speaking to the peasants after the revolt

You wretched men, who seek equality with the lords, are not worthy to live. You will remain in bondage, not as before but harsher.

SOURCE 17 Written by a monk in York in 1399

When the commons saw Wat Tyler was dead they cried out to the King for mercy. The King kindly granted them mercy and ordered two knights to lead the peasants out of London safely so they could go home.

SOURCE 18 From a recent history book

Once the rebels were safely dispersed, the King broke all the promises he had made. All over Essex and Kent, rebel leaders were rounded up and hanged.

SOURCE 19 Written by Sir John Froissart

Later John Ball was found hiding in an old ruin. The King had his [John Ball's] head cut off, as was that of Wat Tyler's, and fixed on London Bridge.

2. Look at Sources 11–19. Which could be used to support Source 9's version of the events, and which to support Source 10's version?
3. Was Richard a coward or was he brave? What do you think about his behaviour?
4. Why do historians today still disagree about what happened at Smithfield?

Scotland victorious, Wales conquered

AS YOU saw on page 66, some parts of the British Isles were claimed by the English King but not under his control.

However, during the Middle Ages the English managed to conquer Wales, but Scotland remained independent. To understand why the Welsh failed where the Scots succeeded we need to look at:

■ the different ways the two countries developed after 1066

■ events during the reigns of Edward I and Edward II.

SOURCE 1 Map of England, Wales and Scotland

Scotland united

Scotland was able to develop peacefully after the Norman conquest of England.

England's kings were not very interested in conquering Scotland. At the time of the Normans it was a poor country, and it was difficult to get to. Some Norman barons were given land in Scotland, but they fitted in well with Scottish landowners, supported the Scottish King and soon became Scottish. Their ability to build strong castles helped to strengthen the Scottish monarchy. The last violent struggle over the Scottish throne was in 1097, and the Scottish kings took control of the whole of Scotland. For a while, during the reign of England's Henry II, the kings of Scotland recognised him as their overlord. But by the time Edward I became King of England in 1272, Scotland was richer and more united than in 1066, and was independent of English control.

Scotland defeats England

In 1286, the Scottish King died without an heir, Edward I of England was asked to decide between the different claims. He expected the king he chose to support him. This did not happen, so in 1296 Edward invaded Scotland, with immediate success. His cavalry seemed to be unbeatable. But although he was able to conquer Scotland, it was difficult to keep it. It was a long way from London, and the mountain area of the Highlands was difficult to keep under control.

The Scots were determined not to be ruled by the English, and led by two great leaders they fought back. The first of these leaders was William Wallace. He was eventually caught by the English, and in 1305 was dragged through the streets of London and then hung, drawn and quartered. His head was stuck on a pike on London Bridge, and his arms and legs were sent to Newcastle, Berwick, Perth and Aberdeen for all to see. However, in the following year the Scots crowned Robert Bruce as their new King and the struggle continued.

An important turning point came in 1307, when Edward I died. His son Edward II was a poor soldier and had no interest in wars with Scotland.

Bruce realised that new tactics were needed and began a brilliant GUERRILLA campaign. He avoided large battles. Small groups of Scots ambushed English soldiers. Castles and crops were destroyed to stop the English using them. The English were forced to withdraw. Edward II at last realised what was happening and sent an army of 25,000 men, including longbowmen, and 3000 heavily armed cavalry. The Scots had only 7000 men and few cavalry, but they were all volunteers and were determined to fight to keep the English out. The two sides met at the Battle of Bannockburn.

In this battle, Bruce again used new tactics, this time to deal with the English cavalry. Scottish foot-soldiers were armed with long pikes and organised into circles, with wooden stakes hammered into the ground in front of them. The heavily-armed English cavalry could not break through, became trapped on boggy ground and were cut down. Meanwhile, the English bowmen were dealt with by the fast-moving and lightly-armed Scottish cavalry.

There was a dreadful slaughter, with the Bannock Burn full of English corpses, which were used by the retreating English as bridges.

The English had to recognise Robert Bruce as the rightful King of Scotland.

▶ **SOURCE 2** Diagram of the battle

▼ **SOURCE 3** Painting of the Battle of Bannockburn, from a fifteenth-century manuscript

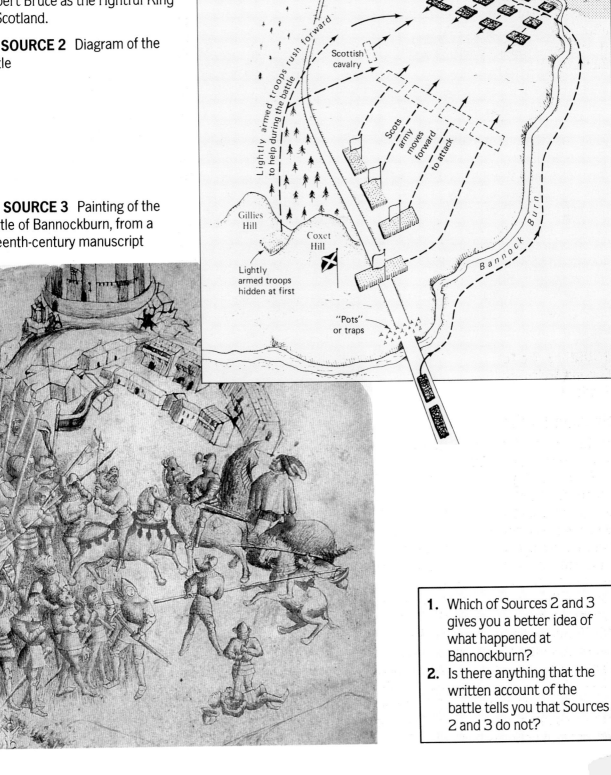

STIRLING CASTLE

English archers

River
Forth

Lightly armed troops rush forward to help during the battle

Scottish cavalry

Scots army moves forward to attack

Gillies Hill

Coxet Hill

Lightly armed troops hidden at first

Bannock Burn

"Pots" or traps

1. Which of Sources 2 and 3 gives you a better idea of what happened at Bannockburn?
2. Is there anything that the written account of the battle tells you that Sources 2 and 3 do not?

Wales is gradually conquered

In the years after 1066 Wales was not united. It consisted of three kingdoms, which were constantly fought over by warring princes. There was no one to unite the country.

Wales is much closer to London than Scotland is, and William I was keen to guard the border with Wales. He gave the borderlands (called the 'Marches') to some of his barons. Over the next 200 years these barons gradually conquered parts of Wales for themselves and strengthened their hold on the country by building castles. They were helped by the arguments between the Welsh princes. Source 4 shows how much of Wales the English controlled by 1150.

However, the Welsh did fight back. Llywelyn the Great, the Prince of Gwynedd, managed to unite the Welsh, and in 1267 his grandson Llywelyn was recognised by the English as 'Prince of Wales'. Even so, by the time Edward I became King of England in 1272, all but the north and west of Wales was under the control of the English barons.

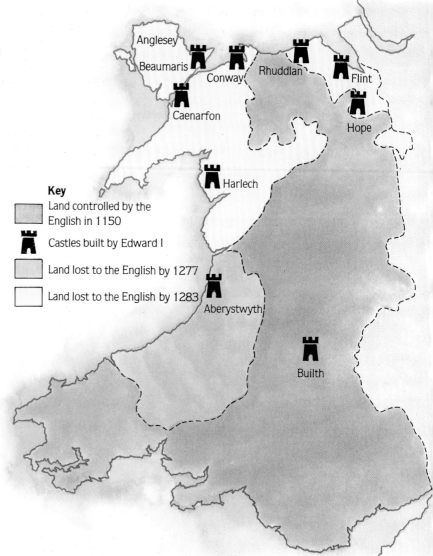

Key

- Land controlled by the English in 1150
- Castles built by Edward I
- Land lost to the English by 1277
- Land lost to the English by 1283

▲ **SOURCE 4** Map of Wales showing areas controlled by the English by 1150

SOURCE 5 Edward I's parliament. Llywelyn, the Prince of Wales, is shown sitting on the right of the King, and Alexander, King of Scotland, on the left

The final conquest of Wales by Edward I

The defeat of the Welsh was partly caused by mistakes by their leader Llywelyn. When Edward I became King of England, Llywelyn refused to support him. Edward decided to conquer Wales, and showed his great military skill and his determination in the conquest.

Llywelyn was let down by the other Welsh leaders and was left to fight by himself, while Edward advanced with three armies, building roads, camps and castles as he went. His navy cut Llywelyn off from his food supplies, which came from the island of Anglesey. Soon Llywelyn was isolated in the north-west corner of Wales and had to surrender.

Llywelyn was allowed to keep his title of 'Prince of Wales' and some of his lands. Then, in 1282, he was persuaded by his brother David to rebel again. They took Edward by surprise, but he gathered together a large well equipped army, which again cut off the Welsh army in the north-west corner of Wales.

Llywelyn and David would probably have been safe from attack there, in their winter stronghold, but Llywelyn took the risk of going south to raise more support. This was a mistake. He was killed while attacking Builth Castle. David was captured in the spring of 1283 and Welsh resistance crumbled.

This time Edward took control of a large part of Wales and made his son Prince of Wales. Wales was divided into counties, like England, and English courts were set up. New castles were also built, to help keep Wales under control, but it wasn't until 300 years later, in 1536, that England and Wales were finally united by the Act of Union.

1. By the time of Edward I large parts of Wales had been conquered, but Scotland had not.
a) How important were particular people in deciding the different outcomes? Get into groups to compare the part played by Robert Bruce in Scotland with that of Llywelyn in Wales. Who was the better leader?
b) Was it important that the Welsh had to fight Edward I, whereas the Scots fought Edward II?

▼ **SOURCE 6** One of Edward's castles in Wales

England – part of Europe?

FOR much of the Middle Ages, England was part of a large Empire. Medieval kings regarded England as only one part, not always the most important, of this Empire.

William I had united Normandy and England in 1066. Henry II (1154–89), a Frenchman, was already Count of Anjou and Duke of Aquitaine before he became King of England in 1154. For a while he even forced the Scottish and Irish kings to recognise him as their overlord. His Empire covered a vast area (see Source 1).

Anjou, not England, was the centre of the Empire and French, not English, was the language used by the King and his nobles. Regular ferry services ran across the Channel between Portsmouth and Southampton in England and Dieppe and Barfleur in Normandy.

Henry and his son Richard I spent nearly all their reigns outside England. Richard spent much of his time, along with the French King, leading armies from all over Europe in a CRUSADE to win back Jerusalem.

As the Middle Ages went on, it was more and more difficult to hold the Empire together. The French kings were determined to conquer those parts of the Empire that had borders with France.

Things came to head during King John's reign. It was much easier for the French kings to concentrate on this struggle than it was for King John. He had big problems in England to worry about, and he found it very difficult to get supplies and orders to his armies across the Channel. By the end of John's reign (1217) only Gascony was left under English control.

Gascony had an important trade with England. Gascony sold wine to England, which in return sold cloth and corn to Gascony. English kings were determined to keep control of Gascony. They also hoped to become kings of France, although it was unlikely they would succeed. It was these two aims that kept the Hundred Years' War with France going from 1337 to 1453.

By 1453 England's only possession on the European mainland was Calais.

---

1. Draw a timeline to show the main stages in England's relationship with France.

SOURCE 1 The Empire in 1154, 1224 and 1453

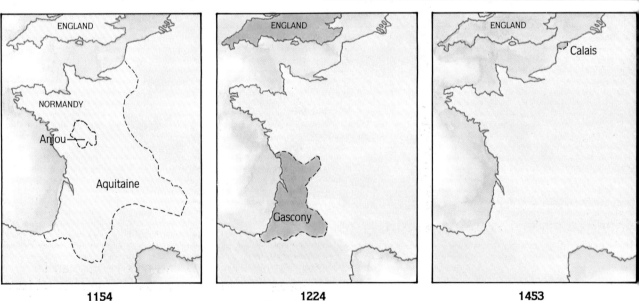

1154　　　　　1224　　　　　1453

Europe's influence on England

In the twelfth century, William of Malmesbury wrote, 'You might see churches rise in every village and town, built in a style unknown before.' Most Saxon churches had been small and simple (see Source 2). Sources 3 and 4 show how church architecture was changed by European styles.

> 1. Describe the main similarities and differences between these three churches. For example, you could comment on the size of the building, the size of the windows, and the building materials used.

SOURCE 2 The Saxon church at Bradford-on-Avon, built in the tenth century

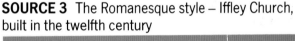

SOURCE 3 The Romanesque style – Iffley Church, built in the twelfth century

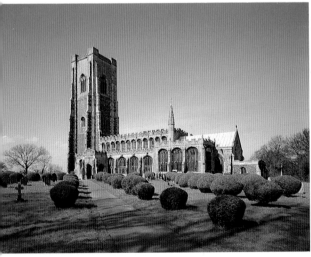

SOURCE 4 The Gothic style – Lavenham Church, built in the fifteenth century

The effects on architecture were obvious for all to see, but involvement in Europe did have other less obvious effects. For example:

■ The heavy taxes needed to pay for the wars with France increased the power of Parliament in England (see page 77).

■ The Poll Tax – also raised to pay for wars in France – helped to trigger the Peasants' Revolt (see page 78).

■ When England finally lost its French lands in 1453, Henry VI became so unpopular in England that he was overthrown. A long struggle for the throne followed between the rival families of Lancaster and York (the 'Wars of the Roses', 1455–1487).

ENGLAND – PART OF EUROPE?

Trade

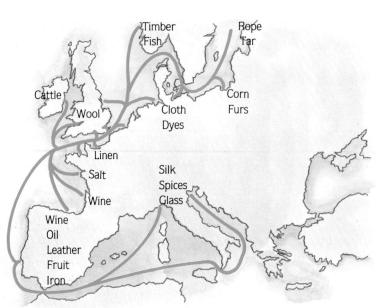

Timber
Fish

Rope
Tar

Cattle

Wool

Cloth
Dyes

Corn
Furs

Linen

Salt

Wine

Silk
Spices
Glass

Wine
Oil
Leather
Fruit
Iron

SOURCE 5 England's main trade routes in the Middle Ages

Contact with Europe affected what the English drank and ate. Early in the Middle Ages ale (beer) was the most popular drink for both rich and poor people, but later the rich drank wine from Gascony, one of England's French lands.

England's involvement in the CRUSADES led to the introduction of many new foods and spices such as pepper, cloves, ginger, almonds, rice, dates, oranges, apricots and melons.

Trade with Europe made a lot of money for the government from customs duties. For example, in 1306, the government had an income of £17,000 from the Gascony wine trade.

The English language

European influences also changed the English language.

Before the Norman Conquest, English was already a mixture of Anglo-Saxon, LATIN, CELTIC and Danish. This mixture can be seen in many English place names.

Place names

The Rivers Avon and Stour have Celtic names (both words simply mean water), while River Cam means crooked.

York and Leeds also have Celtic names, while the Latin 'chester' (meaning fort) was often added to the Celtic to produce names like Manchester and Winchester.

Most place names are either Saxon or Danish. Danish names are common in the north of England, where the Danes settled. Danish endings for place names include '–by' meaning village, '–beck' meaning brook, '–mel' (sand dune), and '–rigg' (ridge).

Saxon endings, found more in the south, include '–burgh' (fort), '–ton' (a village), '–ham' (a farm) and '–mouth' (river mouth), '–ley' (field), and '–stead' (town).

1. Look at a map of your local area. Are Saxon or Danish place names more common?

After 1066 different languages were used for different purposes.
- Most English people – the peasants – carried on using English, although how they spoke it varied between different regions of England.
- Latin was still used in law courts and official documents (such as the Magna Carta) and for services in monasteries and parish churches, as it had been before the Norman Conquest.
- The influence of the Normans meant that French became the language of the lords and the landowners. Some French words gradually became part of the English language.

Words to do with government, such as parliament, justice, court, prison, rent, money, crown, state, council and nation are French; titles, such as prince, duke and baron, are also French.

House is an English word, while manor and palace are French.

Oxen is English, while beef is French.

Many of the older crafts have English names, like baker, miller and shepherd, but newer jobs like mason and tailor are French.

2. How can you tell that the French language was used more by the rich than by the poor?

After the Norman conquest French first names became popular. Names such as Robert, Roger, Maud, Alice and William spread down through society to the peasants. First names from the Bible also became very popular after the Norman Conquest. John was the favourite, but Thomas also became very popular after Becket's murder.

Manorial records from the twelfth century show that only a handful of people had surnames – but 100 years later nearly everyone had one.

They came from parents' christian names (e.g. Nicholson = son of Nicholas), a person's occupation or status (e.g. Thatcher), the place where they lived (e.g. Bridge), or what they were like (e.g. Short).

3. Look at this list of medieval surnames. Decide which come from:
   - parents' names
   - job, occupation or status
   - names of towns or village landmarks
   - appearance or personality.

MILLER	CARTER
LANE	GATES
FRAUNCEYS	YORK
FREEMAN	REEVE
STAFFORD	ATWELL
ROBERTSON	SMITHSON
SMITH	GREY

4. Do the same with some of the surnames of people in your class.

Early in the Middle Ages, English was spoken very differently in different areas and hardly written down at all. But slowly through the centuries an agreed spelling and grammar for English developed as it was used more and more in writing (see Sources 6–8).

Chaucer's *Canterbury Tales* was one of the first great poems to be written in English, in the late 1300s. By the fifteenth century English was replacing both French and Latin as the language of books.

As the Middle Ages went on, more and more people learned to read and write. By the fifteenth century about 30% of the population could do so.

Books became easier to get hold of after the invention of printing in Europe. This spread to England in the 1470s. Caxton, the first English printer, specialised in printing books in English.

5. Sources 6, 7 and 8 show the way written English changed during the Middle Ages. See if you can write any of the three extracts into modern English. Then put the extracts into the correct chronological order.

SOURCE 6

❝She will in no wise receive nor keep your ring with her, and yet I told her that she should not be anything bound thereby; but that I knew by your heart of old that I wist well ye would be glad to forbear the levest thing that ye had in the world, which might be daily in her presence, that should cause her once a day to remember you.❞

SOURCE 7

❝He wæs swyþe spedig man on þæm æhtum þe heora speda on beoþ, þæt is, on wildrum.
He hæfde þagyt, tamra deora unbebohtra syx hund.
He wæs mid þæm fyrstum mannum on þæm lande: næfde he þeah ma þonne twentig hryþera, and twentig sceapa, and twentig swyna.❞

SOURCE 8

❝Withoute bake mete was nevere his hous
of fissh and flessh, and that so plentevous,
it snewed in his hous of mete and drynke,
of all deyntees that men koude thynke.
After the sondry sesons of the yeer,
so chaunged he his mete and his soper.
Ful many a breem and many a luce in stuwe.❞

1. Did England benefit from its contacts with Europe? Draw a line down the centre of your page. On one side write all the advantages of being closely involved in Europe, and on the other side all the disadvantages.

Change and continuity

Which century would you choose to live in?

HERE are some things historians have found out about the different centuries in the Middle Ages.

The twelfth century (1100–1200)
- Landlords in trouble – they have to reduce the labour services of villeins
- Many new churches built
- At end of century, population growing, new land being farmed
- Some towns prosper. Many markets and fairs
- Overseas trade growing
- Prices go up sharply
- Henry II improves system of justice.

The thirteenth century (1200–1300)
- Expansion and prosperity in countryside and towns. Many new towns
- Much trade
- Landowners making money from rents
- Prices stay about the same
- Many beautiful buildings built
- Long periods of civil war
- England not well governed in Henry III's reign.

The fourteenth century (1300–1400)

- Bad famine early in the century
- Heavy taxes for many people
- Peasants' Revolt
- Plague kills many people, but those who survive are better off
- Villages deserted
- Peasants do fewer services for lord of the manor
- Wages go up, and landowners find it difficult to keep workers
- Less trade with Europe because of war.

The fifteenth century (1400–1500)

- Much waste land
- Towns do not grow. No new towns
- Population carries on falling
- Landowners receive low rents
- Prices for farm products very low
- Villages deserted
- A quarter of harvests fail
- Much destruction because of civil wars
- Expensive wars with France, heavy taxes, little trade with Europe
- Ransoms and loot captured from France in wars
- Some signs of things getting better towards end of century, but some towns still in bad state
- Some landowners get rich from sheep farming
- People can afford to eat more meat.

1. Now that you have studied the Middle Ages, which of the descriptions you wrote on page 3 seems most accurate? (You may decide it is a combination of both descriptions.) Give at least five reasons for your answer.

Activity

Divide into three groups:
Group 1 – peasants
Group 2 – lords and ladies of the manor
Group 3 – town shopkeepers and merchants.
Using the information on this page, and what you have learned from the rest of this unit on the Middle Ages, decide which century your group would most like to live in and which century you would least like to live in.

Glossary

AD stands for *Anno Domini* which means 'in the year of the Lord'. It is used for dates after the birth of Christ

Anglo-Saxons people from Germany who ruled England from the fifth century until 1066

archaeologist person who studies past peoples, usually by digging for remains they have left behind, such as buildings or tools. These remains are called **archaeological** evidence

bailiff a medieval manor official appointed by the lord (see **reeve** and **steward**)

baron a powerful lord who was granted land by the King (see **Feudal System**)

BC Before Christ. BC years are counted backwards from the birth of Christ, so 200BC comes before 100BC

bishop a man in charge of the affairs of the Christian Church over a large area called a diocese

boon-work see **week-work**

Celts people living in Britain and northern France before the Romans invaded the area

Charter a medieval document setting out the rights of a town or a group of people

Christendom a collective word for all the countries where Christianity was the main religion, or all the Christians in the world

clergy all the people such as priests, monks, nuns who have been appointed to perform religious duties in the Christian Church

Crusade a holy war to conquer the Holy Land declared by Christians during the Middle Ages

demesne the part of the **manor** farmed by the lord himself in the Middle Ages

Empire the large area of territory controlled by a powerful country

Feudal System the way society was organised throughout Western Europe during the Middle Ages. The King gave land to a small number of powerful men such as barons, knights or lords. In return they supported the King and provided him with an army when he needed one. Ordinary people had to perform various duties for the barons, knights and lords

freeman a peasant who had achieved some freedom from the lord (see **villein**)

guerrilla soldier who fights mainly by ambushes, rather than face to face with the enemy

guild an association of merchants, or workers with a particular craft

Holy Land the area of the Eastern Mediterranean including many places such as Jerusalem which are holy to the Jews, the Christians and the Muslims

Islam the religion based on the teachings of the Prophet Muhammad*. The word Islam means 'submitting', i.e. submitting to God

jury a group of people who hear evidence in a court and decide the verdict

knight a lord who was granted land by a baron in return for support and army service (see **Feudal System**)

Latin official language of the Roman Empire

manor the area controlled by a medieval lord, usually only one village

manuscript handwritten book, often with brightly coloured illustrations

medieval dating from the Middle Ages. In this book, the period called medieval is about AD1000–1500

merchant person who trades in goods, often from foreign countries

peasant the vast majority of poor people in medieval villages, who worked on the land (see **Feudal System**)

pilgrimage journey to a holy place, such as a **shrine**

priest a man in charge of religious ceremonies. In Christian countries, he is responsible for a particular village or parish

reeve a medieval manor official. One of the villagers, and elected by them (see **bailiff** and **steward**)

sheriff official appointed by the King, responsible for keeping law and order in medieval Britain

shrine holy place, usually sacred to a god or a saint

steward official who ran the lord's manor for him in the Middle Ages (see **bailiff** and **reeve**)

succession rules of succession control who will be the next King or Queen of England when the reigning one dies

tithe tax which medieval people had to pay to the village priest: one tenth of their farm produce

Vikings Scandinavians who raided and settled in the south and east of Britain during the ninth and tenth centuries

villein a peasant who was under the control of the lord of the manor in the Middle Ages. A villein could buy his freedom and become a **freeman**

week-work the services, fixed by tradition, that all medieval **villeins** had to give to the lord. **Boon-work** was the extra service the peasant did for the lord when the manor needed it